FEAR GOD

And keep His commandments

Rune Larsen

Copyright

Fear God - And keep His commandments

Published by Author - Rune Larsen

www.SecretRevelations.com

ISBN; 978-82-93411-10-9

Cover design by Panagiotis Lampridis

**'Fear God and keep His commandments.
For this is man's all.
For God will bring every work into
judgement, including every secret thing,
whether good or evil."**

(Ecclesiastes 12:13-14)

Preface

I want this book to be a learning enlightenment book about the fear of the Lord and keeping His commandments.

Making the simplest possible statements that could serve as an anchor for real living faith in the hearts of the humble and sincere of the poor in spirit (Matthew 5:3), which constitutes masses of humanity.

All wisdom - knowledge, begins to fear the Lord
This world's knowledge does not fear God.

Our ministry for the Lord will never grow the right way if we do not begin to fear the Lord.

The spiritual pressure from Satan and the demons world has never been as powerful as it is now in these times.
You, as a Christian, must get into an understanding of how this works, regardless of price.

If you know the Lord, you know your enemies. Are you one of the Lord's sheep will you hear His voice.

In the times we live now, where many optimistic preachers preach a message that is not after Scripture.
It is of great importance in our everyday life: we learn all that we're supposed to do about God's Word.

It is only when we believe and acts on what is written: we will be victorious in Jesus Christ.

This book is written with simple true revelations of the Holy Spirit and contains more than 500 scriptures.
Take your time to read them, and not just skim through.

If you shall obtain a revelation, you must take it yourself. Consequently, read through this book at your normal speed. Incline your ear to the words that are written. That means, in all simplicity, focus, do not let you interfere.

It will be a great pleasure if you get hold of the revelations in this book. Doing so will bring you and your ministry for the Lord into new and compelling revelations.

The Bible

Let the word of Christ dwell in you richly. The divine inspiration of the Scripture is mentioned in the Bible itself.
It is a divine book and the word of God.

"All scripture is given by inspiration of God." (2 Timothy 3:16)

The Word is God, fill yourself constantly with it

"In the beginning was the word, and the word was with God, and the Word was God." (John 1:1)

In this book, it is used scriptures that include the use of the Greek and Hebrew language, to learn in all simplicity the deeper meaning of Scripture.

You are just as important to God as the apostle Paul was
-Never forget that you are one of the Lord's chosen when you have chosen Him.
What you are going to do for the Lord is a part of the universe rescue mission at Calvary Cross.

It always involves bringing people from darkness into light. When you start to stretch out your hands, it will have significant implications for the ones underlying Satan and demons heavy yoke.

Lay down your life, get into a Biblical understanding of how to become victorious in the Lord.
Raise others to victory, be one that teaches God's heavenly revelations to the lost.

You choose whether you will live a life of victory or defeat. It is all up to you.

Grasp the power ministry that the Lord has called you to.

Therefore, go and throw out the rescuing lifebuoys to a sinking people. What you do to the Lord, according to Scripture, will be significant for all eternity.

Intro

Your biblical foundations and actions make way for wisdom and understanding. (Revelations)

Revelations cannot be understood with the reasoning of the mind. The Lord gives them to you.

The key to God's revelations and power is obedience.

A pair of shoes stand on a shoe shelf. These shoes look brand new and without a single scratch. Maybe they are only used from the car and into the 'congregation.'
-It was written on both of these shoes; A hearer of the word.

On the floor under the shoe shelf stands another pair of shoes. These shoes were heavily influenced by field use.
-On these shoes, it was written; A doer of the word. (James 1:22)

Imagine a medieval knight standing there with a 100 lbs armor, and then he lacks his armed shoes?
A soldier in armor without shoes is not very useful in combat. (Ephesians 6:15)
-The slightest blow from the enemy (Satan), and you will fall.

The shoes of the doer, tend to be left out in the 'pastor's' teachings.
There is only one reason for this; He is not interested in going out into the world with the gospel of the Lord, but would rather

stand on his rostrum (a raised platform) and speak out to 'his' hearing sheep.

-All the other parts of the armor, you will not get the hang of if you are not willing to start walking, as the Lord says.

Obedience to what we read is of great importance

When you start taking the Lord seriously, He will respond the same way. If you have not done this in your life, now is the time to do so.

Spend time with the questions in this book. What you learn from it belongs to you. The revelations you get from it, you can give to others. If they do the same as you, suddenly, we are a part of God's people who discipleship others. (Matthew 28:19)

If the Lord says, do this, like this, we must obey from our hearts. If the Lord says; Go out in the whole world with my gospel, we must act on those scriptures.

Sad to say, many believers stay home and begging the Lord day in and day out for an indictment of what to do. If it is written, it is written. If what is written is for us to do, we must do it. If not, we do not believe what the Lord says.

Your first steps in Mark 16:15 feels like walking on water. (Which is a picture of you taking steps in directions that seems impossible for you)

These steps you must make yourself, nobody around you, or in your fellowship, can do it for you.

God does not give you all the understandings upfront, but He promises that signs and wonders shall follow you if you act on what you believe.

I hope you will enjoy and get a lot out of this workbook.

God bless you on your victorious way together with our Lord Jesus Christ.

Author - Rune Larsen

CONTENTS

CHAPTER 1

Fear God

It was night

Somewhere out there; Out there in the spiritual world. The Lord
sat like a General with His elbows firmly placed on His knees,
while gazing at Tellus - the name of our planet. The Lord revealed Himself to me this night - the earth I saw on the left, and
the Lord I saw to the right.

He had full control. His eyes do not depart from earth even a
single second.

This world does not believe in God. It has rejected the Creator
of all things.

Sin reigns, and God's people perish.

The narrow gate

The Bible says that we shall enter by the narrow gate; for wide
is the gate and broad is the way that leads to destruction, and
there are many who go in by it. (Matthew 7:13-14)

This means that we are obliged to find the gate of life, that is a
narrow and steep path when we start walking on it.

‹‹Your life needs to be laid down entirely for the Lord.››

Approximately 150 000 people die every single day
This world does not want to hear about the various individuals who die every day. But instead, they choose to love hearing or watching the news, reporting how a particular celebrity ended his life due to overdosage or jumping out from a window at a five-star hotel.

If people never find the narrow gate, most of them will end up in eternal damnation
This is **not** the will of God Yahweh, who desires all men to be saved and to come to the knowledge of the truth.
(1 Timothy 2:4)

The more disobedient Christians are in obeying the Lord's commandment, which is to go into all the world and preach the Gospel to every creature, the more people will end up in eternal damnation.
Jesus Christ has declared that He will not return before the Gospel has been preached to all the nations.
-Then the end will come.

"And this gospel of the kingdom will be preached in all the world as a witness to all the nations, and then the end will come." (Matthew 24:14)

You must know what to do
People die because of religion. People die from sins. People die without Jesus Christ in their lives.
Begin today to obey the Lord's commandments right now.
-Don't just sit and wait anymore.

"For the wages of sin is death, but the gift of God is eternal life in Christ Jesus, our Lord." (Romans 6:23)

The fear of the Lord is about to disappear

Even if it seems so dark, even if people feel an absolute emptiness - meaninglessness, it is written; "Eternity is in their hearts." (Ecclesiastes 3:11)

They declare that there is no God. But if there were none, then it would not be necessary to proclaim that there were none at all. If you preach repentance from sins and testify that Jesus has been crucified and has risen; There is enough truth in all men to seize the truth. (Ecclesiastes 3:11)

The Lord pays attention to everything that we do and in everything that is going on. Nothing passes Him at any given time. He knows even the number of hair on your head. (Matthew 10:30)

God has total control

"And as it is appointed for men to die once, but after this the judgment." (Hebrews 9:27)

Are you?

Are you continuing to disobey His commandments?
Are you still living a life that is after the lust of the flesh?
Are you still keeping your hands for yourself and refuse to reach your hands to the orphans and the widows?
Are you still declining to preach the Gospel to the lost?
Won't you still make disciples?
Won't you still reach out your hands to anyone?

4

For it is written

"Fear God and keep His commandments, for this is man's all." (Ecclesiastes 12:13)

"For God will bring every work into judgment, including every secret thing, **whether good or evil**." (Ecclesiastes 12:14)

There is no salvation for those who live a life that is after the lust of the flesh. Holiness, together with obedience, must be taken seriously.
Only then will we comprehend who the Lord we serve is.

The uncompromising Spirit

"But the Helper, the Holy Spirit, whom the Father will send in My name, He will teach you all things, and bring to your remembrance all things that I said to you." (John 14:26)

The Holy Spirit goes only in agreement with God's Holy Bible. A revelation in God's word is necessary and will be given unto you when you choose the Lord over the lust of the flesh.

The Bible says

"God our Savior, who desires all men to be saved and to come to the knowledge of the truth." (1 Timothy 2:3-4)

The prince of this world (Satan) has made a complete mess. Different parts of the world are suffering from famine, in other parts reigns materialism. Especially in the richer countries, purchase and discard what applies.

No God they need when they have everything that they 'think' they need.

The spirit of greediness is working feverishly

Everything grows, but your wallet declines. Satan is playing his mind game 24/7. Every day, every week, and every year, he broadcasts his deceiving thoughts to our minds. When God is no longer on man's side, Satan has the freedom to reign and place our lives in misery.

A thought comes

You need a new couch because the old one is not good enough. Then you have this feeling that your couch is an ancient one, so you think that a brand new one is exactly what you need. You agreed to this week's couch sale, and after which it has been delivered to your home, you swipe your shining platinum card, and now you are trapped.

Delusions

Men wearing G-strings and ladies are driving SUV. Believers seek spiritual adventures rather than Almighty God. Starbucks is full of strollers, and women are drinking coffee and chatting most of the day. Pre-made dinners from Walmart are what they bring home.
The Bible shows us the way, not this world's feminists.
The Word of Almighty God always directs our path

Take the Lords commandments serious when He says;

"Do not love the world or the things in the world. If anyone loves the world, the love of the Father is not in him. For all that is in the world-the lust of the flesh, the lust of the eyes, and the pride of life is not of the Father but is of the world." (1 John 2:15-16)

Why follow the world when the Bible reveals what will happen to it?
"And the world is passing away, and the lust of it: but he who does the will of God abides forever." (1 John 2:17)

God's work
The work that the Lord is doing: mankind cannot understand. But the Lord has imposed eternity in our hearts. Then we all have received enough amount of faith to receive salvation through Jesus Christ. (Ecclesiastes 3:11)

When you choose a life that is outside the Lord's commandments, there are no more excuses for it. You choose it. Therefore, the responsibility of your disobedience lies solely on you.

Is God ever angry?
Or is He only a God of love?
God is furious to those who oppose Him every day. To fall in the wrath of God is highly not recommended.

If we think that He is only the God of love, we are for sure wrong. He is not only the God of love but also the God of wrath.

"And do not fear those who kill the body but cannot kill the soul. But rather fear Him (God) who is able to destroy both soul and body in hell." (Matthew 10:28)

Let us see what the Bible says about God is angry or not;

New King James version
"God is a just judge. And God is angry with the wicked every day." (Psalm 7:11)

New International version
"God is a righteous judge. A God who expresses his wrath every day." (Psalm 7:11)

King James version
"God judged the righteous, and God is angry with the wicked every day." (Psalm 7:11)

We read in this verse, the word **wicked**. Wicked is from the Hebrew word; **Räshä.**
Räshä means; Morally wrong, concretely an (actively) bad person, guilty, ungodly, wicked, wicked man that did wrong.

God Yahweh is outraged every single day, enraged on everybody that rebels against His Word - The Holy Bible.

Do you live a life in the work of the flesh and rebel against His commandments? Now it is time to repent and grab what the Lord has for you **before it's too late.**

Nowadays, everybody that is born again must grab everything that the Lord has for them. Satan is working around the clock, tempting all those who believe to fall away from the Lord. **-This we can not accept**.

The power and revelations of the Holy Ghost are the things that we can and must relate to. His power and not on our own. His commandments and not to our own nor from others. **Jesus Christ must be the Lord of all the fields in your life**.

If God is for us, who can be against us? (Romans 8:31)

God has no favor in injustice
"For You are not a God who takes pleasure in wickedness. Nor shall evil dwell with You." (Psalm 5:4)

Doing an act of injustice is an enemy of God.

God hates unjustness
"The boastful shall not stand in Your sight: You hate all workers of iniquity." (Psalm 5:5)

Let's see what King James Bible and the Hebrew language has to say about Psalm 5:5;

"The foolish shall not stand in thy sight: thou hatest all workers of iniquity."

The word; **Iniquity**, is from the Hebrew word: **'aven**.

This means, among other things: Vanity, Malice, specifically an idol, suffering, false, deceitful, evil, grief, injustice, naughty, vain.

It is a big responsibility to be a Christian

The Lord God Almighty has decreed that it is all His born-again children, who shall carry out the great commission, to preach repentance from sin, salvation in Jesus Christ, heal the sick and to cast out demons.

Disobedience is probably only the first name of how believers take this commandment, coming straight from the throne in heaven, where the Lord sits and reigns forever.

"But he who did not know, yet committed things deserving of stripes, shall be beaten with few. For everyone to whom much is given, from him much will be required; and to whom much has been committed, of him, they will ask the more." (Luke 12:48)

God gave us the Holy Ghost

How do we manage this? You are given the Holy Ghost as a helper to teach you all things. (John 14:26)

All things are involved in what Jesus has done for humanity on Calvary.

All things that are necessary for preaching the Gospel to the lost and making disciples.

You confess Jesus as Lord, but is He Lord of all areas in your life? Jesus has chosen all that are willing to follow him, to preach the Gospel to the nations, heal the sick, and to cast out the demons.

You shall love the Lord with all your heart

"You shall love the Lord your God with all your heart, with all your soul, and with all your mind. This is the first and great commandment." (Matthew 22:37-38)

Have you ever grasped what the Lord wants? Not only salvation but His commandments to you?

-We push the Lord away, do we expect that he won't do the same?

"Not everyone who says to Me, Lord, Lord, shall enter the kingdom of heaven, but he who does the will of My Father in heaven." (Matthew 7:21)

Judgment day

The book of Revelation talks about books shall be opened on judgment day, are you aware of this?

When you stand in front of the one who shall open those books, then it is too late to change what has done in your life. Everything that you have done thought and you have said will be judged. **This must be taken seriously now.**

"If we confess our sins, He is faithful and just to forgive us our sins and to cleanse us from all unrighteousness." (1 John 1:9)

"For with God, nothing will be impossible." (Luke 1:37)

"I am the Alpha and the Omega, the Beginning and the End, says the Lord, who is and who was and who is to come the Almighty." (Revelation 1:8)

There is nothing as important in life as this great truth. It will bring us to the cross of Jesus Christ, and drive us to seek and to present every man perfect in Christ Jesus before that great and terrible Day of the Lord comes.

God must be grasped: take it now before it is too late.

Notes;

_____

_____

_____

_____

_____

_____

_____

_____

_____

_____

12

Notes;

_____

_____

_____

_____

_____

_____

_____

_____

_____

_____

_____

_____

CHAPTER 2

Haughtiness

Human's fixed standpoints
We believe that we have authority. We love having the supremacy over all things; Dominating and overcoming the viewpoint of others is such. We tend to manipulate ourselves, as we lift our hands and shout 'Hallelujah' and step on the Lord with our deeds.

"They profess to know God, **but in works they deny Him**, being abominable, disobedient, and disqualified **for every good work**." (Titus 1:16)

Bible says
"You shall not bear false witness against your neighbor."
(Exodus 20:16)

The unbeliever says
There's nothing wrong with white lies.

Yes, you have the Free Will. However, you'll surely pay the price of lying.

14

Bible says

"But the cowardly, unbelieving, abominable, murderers, sexually immoral, sorcerers, idolaters, and all **liars** shall have their part in the lake which burns with fire and brimstone, which is the second death." (Revelation 21:8)

The unbeliever says

It is essential to lie in between; How else can we make it through the day?

Bible says

Go into the world and preach the gospel to every creature.

The unbeliever (disobedient) says

No, that is not my calling.

The Lord says

"But why do you call Me Lord, Lord, and not do the things which I say?" (Luke 6:46)

Today's picture of this world is not difficult to understand: it has severe errors.

"Everyone proud in heart is an abomination to the Lord; Though they join forces, none will go unpunished." (Proverbs 16:5)

We must place ourselves in the hands of the Lord again, and let Him be the one to reign in all the aspects of our lives.

"For if we live, we live to the Lord; and if we die, we die to the Lord. Therefore, whether we live or die, we are the Lord's." (Romans 14:8)

The Bible talks a lot about giving to the poor. We are pro's to give to ourselves.

"He who has pity on the poor lends to the Lord, and He will pay back what he has given." (Proverbs 19:17)

A lot of us are currently not on the right track. We are giving something for us to gain something in return. We thought that we would be blessed just because we blessed others.
This kind of Biblical understanding is a form of haughtiness.

"Do not be deceived, God is not mocked: for whatever a man sows, that he will also reap." (Galatians 6:7)

As a born again, we ought to obey the Lord through His Holy Scripture. You should not follow the desires of your flesh or your selfish wants.

"So let each one give as he purposes in his heart, not grudgingly or of necessity; for God loves a cheerful giver."
(2 Corinthians 9:7)

Fear God who can annihilate everything
"And do not fear those who kill the body but cannot kill the soul. But rather fear Him who is able to destroy both soul and body in hell." (Matthew 10:28)

"For I am the Lord. I speak, and the word which I speak will come to pass; it will no more be postponed; for in your days, O rebellious house, I will say the word and perform it, says the Lord God." (Ezekiel 12:25)

"Heaven and earth will pass away, but My words will by no means pass away." (Matthew 24:35)

"But the word of the Lord endures forever. Now, this is the word which by the gospel was preached to you." (1 Peter 1:25)

This is the Lord Yahweh - The Lord whom you shall face on the judgment day.

"And His mercy is on those who fear Him from generation to generation." (Luke 1:50)

"In mercy and truth atonement is provided for iniquity, and by the fear of the Lord, one departs from evil." (Proverbs 16:6)

"Who shall not fear You, O Lord, and glorify Your name? For You alone are holy. For all nations, shall come and worship before You, for your judgments have been manifested." (Revelation 15:4)

The Free will
The Lord did what seems to us humans impossible. He created us in His image, and He gave us free will. Free will to choose Him or perdition!

There are only two kingdoms; You must decide where you shall belong.
-God does not force anyone.

"God looks down from heaven upon the children of men, to see if there are any who understand, who seek God." (Psalm 53:2)

"For behold, the day is coming. Burning like an oven, and all the proud, yes, all who do wickedly will be stubble. And the day which is coming shall burn them up, says the Lord of hosts, that will leave them neither root nor branch." (Malachi 4:1)

We do not belong to God if we are unavailable for His services. Egoists, self-centered, and spoiled people have no place in His Kingdom.

Notes;

_____

_____

_____

_____

_____

18

Notes;

_____

_____

_____

_____

_____

_____

_____

_____

_____

_____

_____

_____

CHAPTER 3

Rooted in God's word

"As you therefore have received Christ Jesus the Lord, so walk in Him, **rooted** and built up in Him and established in the faith, as you have been taught, abounding in it with thanksgiving." (Colossians 2:6-7)

Imagine a lawn that is watered too much
In this case, the root of the plant doesn't have to work hard in grasping the needed nutrition. These will seem to be floating at the soil due to its water content.
For this cause, the root will be weakened and appears to be useless, for they will no longer exert too much effort in absorbing the nutritious elements that are found in the deeper part of the ground.

The Bible says; Search, seek, knock, ask, and you will find. (Matthew 7:7-8)

On the other side, roots with a moderate amount of water will do the other way around. The roots will work their way down into the soil and grasp the nutrition in it.

The word **rooted** (Colossians 2:6-7) is from the Greek word **rhizoo**, and it means; To become stable, to root.

The illustration mentioned above can be compared to Christians. They had gone, joining from one conference to another, just to feed themselves with insights. Moreover, they will also sit at the same place in 'their' church, and satisfy their selves with the teachings from various pastors.
This results that they will be full of this **kind** of learning.

Unfortunately, after filling their sacks with all this Bible knowledge, they refuse to share it with anyone. They'd choose to close their mouths and tied their feet on the ground every time they refuse to go into the world and preach the Gospel to those who are lost.
-They feel good with their knotted bags, that are fully-stocked with insights. Then they began to transude due to the over-stacked knowledge stored within.

Death is the fruit of their laziness, persecution of their feelings, and ignorance towards the Bible.

"And no one, having drunk old wine, immediately desires new: for he says, **the old is better**." (Luke 5:39)

The Lord wants everybody to learn and know Him
He has endowed us the Holy Ghost for us to fulfill the great mission; To preach the Gospel with power to this world that is lost. Without the Holy Ghost, we remained to have no defense against Satan and the demons.

-If you are baptized with the Holy Ghost, then you have it. The question is; Are you willing to obey?

If you are not willing to obey the Lord's commandments, you will never understand what you are trying to fill yourself with.

"But why do you call Me Lord, Lord, and not do the things which I say?" (Luke 6:46)

Hold on to Christ's commandments

"Now by this, we know that we know Him if we keep his commandments." (1 John 2:3)

"He who says;

I know Him and does not keep His commandments, is a liar, and the truth is not in him. But whoever keeps His word, truly the love of God is perfected in him. By this, we know that we are in Him." (1 John 2:4-5)

Milk is what they want

"For though by this time you ought to be teachers, you need someone to teach you again the first principles of the oracles of God, and you have come to need milk and not solid food." (Hebrews 5:12)

The Bible warns us against the teaching that produces immature Christians.

We fill ourselves with an enormous amount of learning. But most of the teachings are not at the level where it should be. And we are not particularly willing to give unto others, the things that we have learned either.

This results we became such as need milk, not solid food.

"Though He was a Son, yet He learned obedience by the things which He suffered. And having been perfected, He became the author of eternal salvation to all who obey Him." (Hebrews 5:8-9)

"For everyone who partakes only of milk is unskilled in the word of righteousness, for he is a babe." (Hebrews 5:13)

Let's see what the King James version says about the same scripture;
"For everyone that useth milk is **unskilful** in the word of righteousness: For he is a babe." (Hebrews 5:13)

Apeiros, the Greek word for unskilful, it means, inexperienced, ignorant.

More milk
It was a man who once told me that for three years, he had been going to a so-called weekly 'mentoring' with the pastor in a church.
The statement that came was shocking; I do not understand it! The pastor wants to have an hour after the other with me, the same time for every week and three whole years. It is nothing of

what we are talking about that quenches the hunger I have in my heart.

There is no doubt that this certain man should obey God's written word, rather than using this Bible study day to justify his actions for the sake of his pride.

This is the principal paramount problem that the world is facing. Christians, themselves, is not interested in preaching the Gospel to a lost world, but choose to have an emotional charged Sunday in church, and the same in their Bible study throughout the week.

Upon knowing this case, the Bible warns us about this in Hebrews 5:13. Nevertheless, the pastor at this instance must have a sneak in the mirror and reflect what kind of teaching he is doing, and not play the role of a milk producer and a controlling manipulator.

-Let the Bible study day be what it is, nothing else.

Jesus gave His life on the cross for all our sins

Then here comes a question which you have to answer in front of the Lord; Given the fact that Jesus has chosen all the Christians to preach to every creature, well, who do you think these Christians are? Is it the Evangelist? Is it the Pastor? Is it the Prophet? Is it the Apostle? Or is it the Teacher? Or is it all those who sit in a 'church' every Sunday, that have no idea what their call is?

You must have the understanding for you to comprehend spiritual facts. If you do not percept the will of God, then you'd probably believe an infidel who says something else.

Here an example of what I have experienced, which is in similar cases; My wife and I were at dinner with some acquaintances. I urged to talk as usual about the Lord's mission commandment. The commandment is to go into the entire world with His Gospel.
-Then it comes.
We travel nowhere until the Lord tells us precisely where we should go.
-But He did already through the Bible.
No, God must tell us first, not an inch we go before that happens!

What shall you respond to these statements?
-The first is; They are not willing to go into the world with the Gospel of the Lord.
-The second is; There is absolutely no distress for the will of the Lord in their lives. They remained to be self-centered and selfish people as they could ever be.

What is written in Mark 16:15?
"Go into all the world and preach the gospel to every creature."

The country where you are in is a part of the whole world.

Jesus died for all the sinners, and who will be out and be a witness of salvation's message? All Christians!

The Bible says

The Holy Ghost shall teach you all things, and what includes within all these things? To preach the Gospel to the lost, to heal the sick, to make disciples (followers), and to cast out demons. If we do not start to walk down that path, then the Holy Ghost cannot learn you much.

The discernment between spirits will not evolve much also because we are not out there where we need to discern.

We will not have much understanding of what the Lord wants to do for the sick.

A big part of God will be missed because we are disobedient.

Let the word of God dwell abundantly in you

"Let the word of Christ **dwell** in you richly in all wisdom, teachings, and admonishing one another in psalms and hymns and spiritual songs, singing with grace in your hearts to the Lord." (Colossians 3:16)

The word **dwell** is from the Greek word: **eneikeo**. It means; To inhabit, dwell in.

We shall live in God's word the way we live in our houses, which we are all familiar with in the nooks and crannies and the storage of our things. Likewise, we must thoroughly put us into the word. God's word must be as familiar to us as all our rooms in our homes.

God's word must inhabit us. This is much more than just reading the Bible.

If it is written, it will be like that

The Lord says we are in a war - Which you have to believe.
Otherwise, you'll lose.

The Lord says that no sinner will inherit His Kingdom.

-Why do you continue to live under carnal desires?

God's true infallible written word

"But the word of the Lord endures forever. Now, this is the word
which by the Gospel was preached to you." (1 Peter 1:25)

"All Scripture is given by inspiration of God, and is profitable
for doctrine, for reproof, for correction, for instruction in righteousness, that the man of God may be complete, thoroughly
equipped for every good work." (2 Timothy 3:16-17)

"This book of the Law shall not depart from your mouth, but
you shall meditate on it day and night, that you may observe to
do according to all that is written in it. For then you will make
your way prosperous, and then you will have good success."
(Joshua 1:8)

The Lord wants us to bend our ear to His Word

How we live in this world today, have taught us and listen to
two things at once. The TV is on, and at the same time, we read
the Bible. There is music to our ears when we pray.

Much of the disturbances we take for 'good' fish, and just accept
it. **This works badly.**

To focus on what the Bible says, will not be easy. We think that what we do is right, but we seldom or never come into that intimate communion with the Lord, including hearing His voice.

"My son, give attention to my words: **incline your ear** to my sayings. Do not let them depart from your eyes: keep them in the midst of your heart: for they are life to those who find them. And health to all their flesh." (Proverbs 4:20-22)

There are four directions which one must follow
Let's take a look closer to what is written in Proverbs 4:20-22.

1. Give attention to my words (4:20)
Often we read the word of God with our attention that is divided. Our minds are preoccupied with this world. This causes the word of God to become unfruitful. We must shut out the things of this world, and give our full attention to God.

"Now he who received seed among the thorns is he who hears the word, and the cares of this world and the deceitfulness of riches choke the word, and he becomes unfruitful."
(Matthew 13:22)

2. Incline your ear to my sayings (4:20)
An inclined ear implies an attitude of spiritual hunger and humility. Stubbornness and disbelief limit the impact of the word of God in our lives. Jesus warned us against human traditions that make God's commandments to nothing.

Traditional religious ideas, prejudices, and preconceptions prevent the word of God in all things.

(More information in Colossians 2:8)

-Therefore, we must always be open and hungry for God's word.

3. Do not let them depart from your eyes (4:21)

It is essential to keep both eyes completely fixed on God's
promises.

A doubtful Christian must not expect to receive anything from
the Lord. (James 1:7-8)

Focus on God's word with unshaken faith.

4. Keep them in the midst your heart (4:22)

Give time to God's Word, for it has the power to affect the lives
of our souls and health to our meat.

"For they are life to those who find them, and health to all their
flesh." (Proverbs 4:22)

Go ahead, be shameless in prayer

In the Gospel of Luke, Chapter 11, verse 1:13, we read about
how Jesus teaches the disciples to pray.

Let us first read Luke 11:8 from the King James Bible;
I say unto you, though he will not rise and give him because he
is his friend, yet because of his **importunity**, he will rise and
give him as many as he needeth.

Let us consider only a single word of all the 13 verses.

In verse 8, we read: because of his **importunity**. Importunity is from the Greek word **anaideia**.

The word: anaideia, involves an element of insistence that rises to the point of shamelessness, which the English word: importunity, are unable to express. This <u>reduces</u> the argument of the parable, which is: if shameless insistence, favor can be won. Even from an unwilling and rude/unfriendly behavior.
How is your prayer life? Do you dare to be shameless in prayer?

Everything has to be rooted in God's written Word, the Bible
If it is not connected to the Bible, it is spiritual words from Satan and the demons.
-The mystery of God has all roots in God's written Word, the Bible.

God's written Word is meant to be preached to the world, for the world's freedom in Jesus Christ.

"And you shall know the truth, and the truth shall make you free." (John 8:32)

Listen to what Paul says in Ephesians;
"That utterance may be given to me, that I may open my mouth boldly to make known the mystery of the gospel."
(Ephesians 6:19)

Believe it - Take it - Became a winner in Jesus Christ.

This world's wisdom and traditions are not of the Lord
"Beware lest anyone cheat you through philosophy and empty deceit, according to the tradition of men, according to the basic principles of the world, and not according to Christ."
(Colossians 2:8)

There is only one way, and that is not this world's traditional way.

"Jesus said to him;
I am the way, the truth, and the life. No one comes to the Father except through Me." (John 14:6)

Notes;

_____

_____

_____

_____

_____

_____

_____

_____

CHAPTER 4

Keep His commandments

Born again but disobedient

Nowadays, disobedience to the Lord's commandments reigns unto the believers. Most of them don't want to go out in the world, with the Gospel of Jesus Christ. Others think it is only the evangelist who shall preach around the world, and many do not want anything to do with the Lord's commandments.

Jesus will return when all the nations have been given the gospel

"And this gospel of the kingdom will be preached in all the world as a witness to all the nations, and then the end will come." (Matthew 24:14)

When Jesus <u>returns</u>, it is either heaven or hell.

This is a wonderful promise, and we must rejoice upon this. Unfortunately, people are just too busy for themselves.

The harvest is plentiful, but where are the workers?

"Then He said to His disciples, the harvest truly is plentiful, but the laborers are few." (Matthew 9:37)

All of them want to go to heaven

But they might not be prepared 'right' now. Perhaps, they will be when they have earned and used the first million dollars, and hunt the next one excitedly. But this time, the hunt is on with invested equipment, for 'only' 20% interest.

Why is it we find it hard to begin?

Everything starts with one thing - Who is your Lord?
You just can't proclaim that Jesus is your Lord when your daily life is all about getting most into your kingdom.

Don't let yourselves to be conformed to this world, says the Lord

"And do not be conformed to this world, but be transformed by the renewing of your <u>mind</u>, that you may prove what is good and acceptable and perfect will of God." (Romans 12:2)

As believers, what are we doing then?

Why are we not keeping on going with everything which we can contribute with if the Lord wants to fellowship with us with all His heart?

Look at the enormous promise in John 14:26

-The Holy Spirit will teach you all things.

Nevertheless, there is an 'if' to this Scripture; If you are not willing to go unto the place where God wants to use you, then what is the purpose of learning all the things from the Holy Spirit?

-Or do you want it because you wish to be someone who gives everything to others?

A ministry for the Lord involves a simple thing; Give to others.

Are you the one who goes to church on Sunday, working Monday-Friday, sometimes Saturdays, plus overtime, and then going camping or other trips on the weekends? Then it is very little time left for the Lord and His commandments.

Raise your daily cross
The time has come for us, Christians, to take a look in the mirror seriously. And when you look at your reflection from the mirror, do not only think of what you see and feel, but rather think of what the Lord says, and the plans He has for you here on earth and in heaven.

God's written Word; The Bible
"Then He said to them all if anyone desires to come after Me, let him deny himself and take up his cross daily and follow me." (Luke 9:23)

Work needs to begin here
Salary chamber, repentance, obeying the mission commandment, holiness, and a daily breakdown of the flesh's desires. Seek the Lord, not this world.

-You shall love your neighbor as yourself. (Matthew 22:39)

-Go into all the world and preach the Gospel to every creature. (Mark 16:15)

Grab it now! Don't wait any longer.

Fear God and keep His commandments. For this is man's all. (Ecclesiastes 12:13)

All shall become a witness
If you believe that you do not have a calling to be a; Preacher, a Prophet, a Shepard, a Teacher others, then you shall be a witness, and that's for sure.
-Here it all begins.

The message of repentance to the sinful world
This is what we ought to do. We are called to declare the wonderful message of Jesus' death, was crucified, and was risen.

"For if anyone is a hearer of the word and not a doer, he is like a man observing his natural face in a mirror; for he observes himself, goes away, and immediately forgets what kind of man he was." (James 1:23-24)

Excuses that fails
"Then Moses said to the Lord, O my Lord, I am not eloquent, neither before nor since You have spoken to Your servant, but I am slow of speech and slow of tongue. So the Lord said to him, who has made man's mouth? Or who makes the mute, the deaf, the seeing, or the blind? Have not I, the Lord? Now, therefore,

go, and I will be with your mouth and teach you what you shall say." (Exodus 4:10-12)

We use excuses like this; I'm not good with words

We seem to escape from our obligation, which is to share the Gospel to a lost world. This is a sin against He who gave you your voice.

Listen;

"Also I say to you, whoever confesses me before men, him the Son of Man also will confess before the angels of God. But he who denies Me before men will be denied before the angels of God." (Luke 12:8-9)

Jesus must be the only cornerstone. Otherwise, it compromises.

They gave what they had

Two men in India are burning zealous in the Lord's service. One was blind but is healthy, the other was paralyzed from the waist and downwards. They had an old bike as they rode around with every day. The blind one sat on the luggage rack and trodden the bicycle, the other one who was paralyzed, sat on the seat with his feet hanging over the handlebars and controlled the bike.
In this situation, we can see two men with a significant handicap.
But they were on fire for the Lord. They rode around and preached the Lord's Gospel. What characterized their ministry was both of them functioned powerfully in healing. They had small and large campaigns around in India.

When they could not use the bicycle, the blind carried the paralyzed.

This is an awesome testimony that all things are possible in the mighty name of Jesus.

The Bible says
"And these signs will follow those who believe; In My name, they will cast out demons; they will speak with new tongues; they will take up serpents; and if they drink anything deadly, it will by no means hurt them; they will lay hands on the sick, and they will recover." (Mark 16:17-18)

Although you might have a handicap, it does not and will not prevent the Lord to use you powerfully.
It's all up to you. Dare to believe it - Act on it!

While you believe the Lord for your healing, go and preach the Gospel where you are, and the Lord will be with you.

Have all the focus on the Lord
"But seek first the kingdom of God and His righteousness, and all these things shall be added to you." (Matthew 6:33)

What you see in yourself that is weak from the sight of others, the Lord will use for His Glory.

"But God has chosen the foolish things of the world to put to shame the wise, and God has chosen the weak things of the

world to put to shame the things which are mighty."
(1 Corinthians 1:27)

If you just believe God's word, and act on it; It will work
"Thus also faith by itself, if it does not have works, is dead."
(James 2:17)

Do not look at the circumstances: keep your eyes on the Lord.
He is the Alpha and the Omega, the creator of the timeline. And
you are a part of it.

Relate to the Biblical facts
Believe it, act on it - and see God in action through you.

Are you born again? Then get going
"As you, therefore, have received Christ Jesus the Lord, so walk
in him, rooted and built up in Him and established in the faith,
as you have been taught, abounding in it with thanksgiving. Beware lest anyone cheat you through philosophy and empty deceit, according to the tradition of men, according to the basic
principles of the world, and not according to Christ."
(Colossians 2:6-8)

Fill yourself with Jesus Christ
What your heart flows over with, your mouth speaks.
(Luke 6:45)

Meditate and live with His Word, all day, every day
"This book of the Law shall not depart from your mouth, but
you shall meditate on it day and night, that you may observe to

do according to all that is written in it. For then you will make your way prosperous, and then you will have good success." (Joshua 1:8)

Look at the enormous promise at the end of this verse; it will make your way prosperous, and then you will have good success.

There is victory in Jesus name
The same power that has raised Jesus from the dead dwells in you.
When you were baptized in the Holy Ghost, you got a full tank. Start to pray for the sick, cast out demons, and heal the sick. Be God's rescue arm as a part of the universe's biggest rescue mission on Calvary.

"But if the Spirit of Him who raised Jesus from the dead dwells in you, He who raised Christ from the dead will also give life to your mortal bodies through His Spirit who dwells in you." (Romans 8:11)

They are all waiting, what are you waiting for?
If you are one of those who do not believe that you have a calling to preach the Gospel, then consider the following; there is a page after page in the Bible about reaching out our hands to the needy. We have no coverage in the Scripture that someone who is born again shall not perform this.

"These things I command you, that you love one **another.**" (John 15:17)

Allelon, the Greek word for **another**. It means; The others.
-Who are the others? Everybody else, all the people, all the sick, all the poor, all the afflicted.

Taking care of widows
Very specific, the Lord has written in the Bible about the widows. Have you ever thought about this? In heaven, there are no widows. Then it is for you and me to do something with it now. (More info in James 1:27)

Children
Many organizations collect money to feed hungry children around the world. Why is not the general Christian doing the same?
There is no place in the Scripture when we are making disciples: they will only be in a specific age group.

God is near the poor
"He who has pity on the poor lends to the Lord. And He will pay back what he has given." (Proverbs 19:17)

Very much Christianity is selfishness
We think only of ourselves. We ask God for the things for our self, while elsewhere in the world do have neither shoes nor pants. They are born, live, and die on the sidewalks. People live in dumpsites.
-We have enough of the things mostly.

Yahweh is;
"He has delivered us from the power of darkness and conveyed us into the kingdom of the Son of His love." (Colossians 1:13)

The Quintessential Father. (Matthew 5:48)

Give thanks to God Yahweh
"Giving thanks always for all things to God the Father in the name of our Lord Jesus Christ." (Ephesians 5:20)

You must live in His presence
"Who comforts us in all our tribulation, that we may be able to comfort those who are in any trouble, with the comfort with which we ourselves are comforted by God." (2 Corinthians 1:4)

"He who overcomes shall inherit all things, and I will be his God, and he shall be my son." (Revelation 21:7)

I am the Alpha and the Omega, the Beginning and the End. I will give of the fountain of the water of life freely to him who thirsts. (Revelation 21:6)

Our heavenly Father; He wants to have a fellowship with me and you forever. Think about it.
Almighty God, who knows everything that you have said, done and thought. He wants you to come to Him.

The Bible says
We are created in His image. (Genesis 1:27)
Heavenly Father, I thank you in Jesus' Name. (Ephesians 5:20)

CHAPTER 5

Pride

Pride prevents the Holy Spirit from working in you
Everything that has to do with pride is a devastating enemy. Do everything you can to get rid of it.

The Lord cannot teach you much when you cling to your pride
You can choose whether to cuddle with pride, like a soft fur coat that hangs around your neck or use that pride in judging others with their errors, instead of admitting your own. You can choose to grab the whole pride and throw it far into the sea so that you can never see it again. Or you can continue to treat it as your most precious asset.

The Lord is not at all with the proud. But if you humble yourself, He is there with all His Grace.

Why do you want to stay with your pride when it leads only to one thing?

"A man's pride will bring him low, but the humble in spirit will retain honor." (Proverbs 29:23)

"When **pride** comes, then comes **shame**. But with the humble is wisdom." (Proverbs 11:2)

The word **pride** is from the Hebrew word **zadown**. It means; Arrogance, presumptuously, pride, proud.

The next word in Proverbs 11:2 is perhaps one of the most important words when it comes to pride, and what will happen when we let pride into our lives and decisions.
-We read the word **shame**. Shame is from the Hebrew word **qalown**. It means; Dishonor, shame, **confusion**.

Let us reread Proverbs 11:2, and this time with a revelation; When you use pride in your life - actions, confusion will follow right away.

Here is one of the main causes why believers do not want to preach the gospel to the lost. Many let pride controls their emotional decisions instead of God's word. When you adapt confusion to your life as a believer, it will be hard to enter into an understanding of who the Lord is and what He wants.

Pride
I have confronted people with their pride many times. And most of the time, I have been faced with denials: No, I don't have any pride - Never! - I am certainly not - Pride? - I never had pride - If I have pride, how can I be saved then?

If you have taken a settlement with pride, then different statements will be coming out of your mouth.

What shall we do to understand how pride is working in our lives fully? Seek first the kingdom of God. Not your feelings or other infidel people's opinions.

"You shall love the Lord your God with all your heart, with all your soul, and with all your mind." (Matthew 22:37)

Pride, the biggest obstacle to entering what the Lord has and wants for you
In my own life, I have fought against pride many times. As I became more familiar and closer to the Lord, I have received many revelations about how much pride had hindered me in my life.

I will not go into details about this for now, but what can be said, is what you may be not perceived as pride, it is a chance it is. To live a life surrendered to the Lord is the first step that must be taken.

Full surrender
No compromise whatsoever on God's written Word.

Pride prevents you from entering the talents that the Lord has placed in you
God has given us all talents. You will not be able to discover your talents if you are not willing to die from yourself.
All sin must cease: all pride and arrogance must cease. Your quiet time with the Lord, your Bible reading, must become a priority every single day. **All pride must be destroyed in your life**.

Pride prevents you from understanding

If you never can enter what the Lord has for you, it is a chance that you became someone who is just rambling along with others, with little or no goals or opinions.

Entire nations are under the yoke of pride.

If you're proud, then you use **all** the excuses that exist, only to justify your actions rather than anything else. What happens when you genuinely humble yourself before the Lord? That is when the real redemption of what He has for you will begin. This is where you will start to understand what the Lord wants with you.

God has set a day overall proud

"For the day of the Lord of hosts shall come upon everything proud and lofty. Upon everything lifted up, and it shall be brought low." (Isaiah 2:12)

God can't stand proud eyes

"Whoever secretly slanders his neighbor, him I will destroy? The one who has a haughty look and a proud heart, him I will not endure." (Psalm 101:5)

Many claims to be a Bible reader;

-Do you read the Bible?
Yes, of course!
-When did you read it last time?
Ahh, I can't remember.

-Do we find your answer Biblically correct according to Scripture?

I read the Bible!

-Yes, you say so, but is your study of the word of the Lord according to scripture?

Maybe!

-Well, then I can inform you that it is not. You can begin by reading what is written in Joshua 1:8.

When a believer's life is as stated above, the doer of the word is not at all in position in our life.

Firstly, you use your pride to justify your way of reading the Bible. Then fails to answer one of the questions here, by pointing out your Bible reading.

The fruit of pride brings nothing else than bad fruits. Bad fruit to yourself and others. To humble yourselves and be honest in this case, had not been difficult. Yet chooses people to use pride rather than honesty. This leads quickly to lies.

They lied utterly unnecessary. It cost them their lives

"But a certain man named Ananias, with Sapphira, his wife, sold a possession. And he kept back part of the proceeds, his wife also being aware of it, and brought a certain part and laid it at the apostle's feet." (Acts 5:1-2)

Often in our lives, we lie

The Bible says that we should not lie, either 'black or white.' Satan fills us with thoughts. You accept these thoughts because you do not know how to bring them into captivity.

The thoughts that are accepted leads many times into a lie, further in death as in Acts 5:1-5.

Ananias arrived with a part of the sum, and let it at the apostle's feet

"But Peter said, Ananias, why has Satan filled your heart to lie to the Holy Spirit and keep back part of the price of the land for yourself? While it remained, was it not your own? And after it was sold, was it not in your control? Why have you conceived this thing in your heart? You have not lied to men but to God." (Acts 5:3-4)

The punishment for lying to the Spirit of God

"Then Ananias, hearing these words, fell down and breathed his last." (Acts 5:5)

His wife knew about it, and she received the same penalty

Three hours after her husband had died, she suddenly came. Peter said to her; tell me whether you sold the land for so much? She said yes for so much. Then Peter said to her, how is it that you have agreed together to test the Spirit of the Lord? Look, the feet of those who have buried your husband are at the door, and they will carry you out. Then immediately she fell at his feet and breathed her last. And the young men came in and found her dead, and carrying her out, buried her by her husband." (Acts 5:7-10)

All your deeds, you are responsible for

"For God will bring every work into judgment. Including those secret things, whether good or evil." (Ecclesiastes 12:14)

The daily breakdown of yourself

The daily breakdown of yourself is one of the most critical aspects of the Christian life. Our flesh, Satan, everything that stands between you and the Lord, must be taken seriously and be fought.

"Your word is a lamp to my feet and light to my path."
(Psalm 119:105)

The Lord, our God, comes with a severe warning in this passage

"I will punish the world for its evil, and the wicked for their iniquity. I will halt the arrogance of the proud, and will lay low the haughtiness of the terrible." (Isaiah 13:11)

Notes;

_____

_____

_____

_____

_____

_____

_____

48

Notes;

CHAPTER 6

God's 10

God's 10 Commandments - our conscience.

The first and the second commandment says; You shall have only one God, and you shall have no idols.

It is an abomination in the sight of the Lord to see that His children turn to dumb idols.

1st commandment
"You shall have no other gods before Me." (Exodus 20:3)

2nd commandment
"You shall not make for yourself a carved image - any likeness of anything that is in heaven above, or that is in the earth beneath, or that is in the water under the earth; you shall not bow down to them nor serve them. For I the Lord your God, am a jealous God, visiting the iniquity of the fathers upon the children to the third and fourth generations of those who hate Me. But showing mercy to thousands, to those who love me and keep my commandments." (Exodus 20:4-6)

In the Old Testament, we can see that the people made several types of idols with all the varieties and sizes.

But is it any different today?

People are living in what we call civilized homes. They pull perhaps not out their gold teeth and melt and hammer together a gold calf and bow down to it in their living room. But in the same living room, it is carried out many things that are entirely in line with to make a golden calf, as they did when Moses received the 10 Commandments.

Football, they are crazy after it

Most homes have a huge flat screen on the wall, and a table filled with alcohol on the big day. The day in which 'them' football match will take its place.

Imagine a football game, in the stands sitting thousands of supporters. They have their favorite themes colors on their clothes, and many are painted likewise in their faces. A football supporter in full gear at the stands does not look much different than a thousand-year-old Inca priest who sacrificed humans to idols. Whether they are sitting on the football stands, or in their homes, idol worshipping is performed the same way.

Catholicism is one of the religions that openly worship idols and justifies it. Hindus have millions of idols. The greedy, they are not interested in anything else than their prosperity and multiplying it.

"They exchanged the truth of God for the lie, and worshipped and served the creature." (Romans 1:25)

What do those who confess to be believers, but denies the Lord's commandments?

-Their pride is their idol.

Here is the list endless. It can be written books about human pride against Jesus Christ and His commandments.

"They profess to know God, but in works they deny Him, being abominable, disobedient and disqualified for every good work." (Titus 1:16)

There is only one way to heaven with our prayers and actions.

"Jesus said to him, I am the way, the truth, and the life. No one comes to the Father except through Me." (John 14:6)

"And whatever you do in word or deed, do all in the name of the Lord Jesus, giving thanks to God the Father through Him." (Colossians 3:17)

3rd commandment

"You shall not take the name of the Lord your God in vain, for the Lord will not hold him guiltless who takes His name in vain." (Exodus 20:7)

Are you swearing in the Lord's Name?

Like;

Oh, my g*d! JES*S! For g*d sakes! JES*S CHRIST! H*ly Sh*t! God d*mn! For hea*ens sake! And so on.

Let's have a look at the word **vain**, in Exodus 20:7. Vain is from the Hebrew word shav´, and it means; In the sense of desolating: evil (as destructive), literally ruin, uselessness, in vain - false(-ly), lie, **lying**, vain, **vanity**.

Here we see that if you swear in His name, you have sinned and make the Lord's name to nothing.

When you swear using anything that has to do with the Lord, you are standing nose to nose with Almighty God, and you tell Him that He is nothing - He is vain, a zero!

We also see from the Hebrew word **vain**, that it also means **lying**. When you speak God down to nothing, **you are lying**.

Is it strange that He says at the end of this Commandment; For the Lord will not hold him guiltless who takes His name in vain? If you do not remember what Revelation 21:8 says about lying, please look it up.

For out of the abundance of the heart, his mouth speaks. (Luke 6:45)

Any abuse of the Lord's Name must come to an absolute end in our lives.

Do you have illicit work?
Maybe you have donated some money to a Christian - Humanitarian project, and then post it on Facebook where you give thanks to the Lord for the blessings.

This money that you are trying to justify is to take the Lord's Name in vain. Why? Illicit work is stolen tax money. To give God the glory for stealing is not very advisable.

Countless religions use the name, Jesus

Anyone who does not use it according to scripture, the Lord our God will hold responsible for misusing His Name.

If you understand what is written here, go and warn those around you to stop taking the Lord's name in vain.
-I am sure you will have plenty of work.

4th Commandments

"Remember the Sabbath day, to keep it holy. Six days you shall labor and do all your work, but the seventh day is the sabbath of the Lord your God. In it, you shall do no work; you, nor your son, nor your daughter, nor your male servant, nor your female servant, nor your cattle, nor your stranger who is within your gates. For in six days the Lord made the heavens and the earth, the sea and all that is in them, and rested the seventh day. Therefore, the Lord blessed the Sabbath day and hallowed it."
(Exodus 20:8-11)

Let us read verse 9 in the King James Bible; "Six days shalt thou labor, and do all thy **work**." (Exodus 20:9)

The word work, is from the Hebrew word **mla´kah**, and it means; Ministry, a messenger of God.

When it comes to our daily work, of course, it has to be 5-6 days a week, plus overtime and boat trips at the weekends. Apart from a few holiday weeks, then we travel somewhere to relax and enjoy ourselves.

We shall maximize our effectiveness in all that we are doing. We work for this world from early in the morning, too late in the evening.

Keeping the Sabbath?

As born-again believers in the new covenant, we shall not keep the Sabbath. But if you want to rest one day a week, do it.

Jesus requires everything

"But why do you call Me Lord, Lord, and not do the things which I say?" (Luke 6:46)

Man does not want God. They do not want to obey God. They choose to put their trust in the same work as this world does. First, my self, only mine, and some more to myself.

5th Commandments

"Honor your father and your mother, that your days may be long upon the land which the Lord your God is giving you." (Exodus 20:12)

This is the first commandment with a promise.

This world's fifth commandment, rebellion against parents, is; Resistant.

The Bible says; Honor your father and your mother.

6th Commandments

"You shall not murder." (Exodus 20:13)

When we have read this passage, most of us are thinking; Did I kill someone? Of course, No. I have never done that, and I will never do it either.

If we read in the Gospel of Matthew, we can see that the Lord has a different perception of what killing is.

Jesus warns us that if we get angry without a cause, then we were in danger of the judgment.

"But I say to you that whoever is angry with his brother without a cause shall be in danger of the judgment. And whoever says to his brother, Raca! Shall be in danger of the council. But whoever says, you fool! Shall be in danger of hell fire."
(Matthew 5:22)

We can violet God's law by our attitude and our fleshy intent.

"Whoever hates his brother is a murderer, and you know that no murderer has eternal life abiding in him." (1 John 3:15)

"But the cowardly, unbelieving, abominable, murderers, sexually immoral, sorcerers, idolaters, and all liars shall have their part in the lake which burns with fire and brimstone, which is the second death." (Revelation 21:8)

Do you see yourself here? If so, repent to the Lord right away.

56

7th commandment
"You shall not commit adultery." (Exodus 20:14)

Who among us can say that we are pure in heart?
Jesus warned the people: You have heard that it was said in old times, thou shall not commit adultery.
But I say unto you verily that whosoever looketh at a woman with lust to her, then he has already committed adultery with her in his heart.

We read the whole passage in the Gospel of Matthew;
"But I say to you that whoever **looks** at a woman to lust for her has already committed adultery with her in his heart."
(Matthew 5:28)

"For this you know, that no fornicator, unclean person, nor covetous man, who is an idolater, has any inheritance in the kingdom of Christ and God." (Ephesians 5:5)

This world's 7th Commandment; Adultery is dating.

God has seen every thought you have had and every sin you have committed.

"You know my sitting down and my rising up; you understand my thought afar off. You comprehend my path and my lying down, and are acquainted with all my way." (Psalm 139:2-3)

"For my eyes are on all their ways; they are not hidden from My face, nor is their iniquity hidden from My eyes." (Jeremiah 16:17)

The day will come wherein you will face His law.
The Bible says that the impure and fornicators will not enter the Kingdom of God. The penalty for violating this commandment is the death penalty.

Repent and believe the Gospel. (Mark 1:15)

8th commandment

"You shall not steal." (Exodus 20:15)

Big or small; There must be no stealing. This also includes file sharing and downloading of copyrighted material, such as software, movies, and music.

9th commandment

"You shall not bear false witness against your neighbor." (Exodus 20:16)

We read the word **false**. It is from the Hebrew word **sheqer**, and it means; An untruth, a sham often without a cause, deceitful, false, falsely, liar, lie, lying, vain, wrongfully.

Choose to live your life following God's way, not in this world's way

"Do not love the world or the things in the world. If anyone loves the world, the love of the Father is not in him."
(1 John 2:15)

Do not lie to each other

"Do not lie to one another, since you have put off the old man with his deeds, and have put on the new man who is renewed in knowledge according to the image of Him who created him."
(Colossians 3:9-10)

"He who works deceit shall not dwell within my house. He who tells lies shall not continue in my presence." (Psalm 101:7)

What Jesus has told us to do must prevail.
"Come to Me, all you who labor and are heavy laden, and I will give you rest." (Matthew 11:28)

The Bible warns

All the liars shall have their part in the lake of fire. Maybe you thought that a little bit dishonesty and some white lie here and there is not a serious sin?
-God does.

"The truthful lip shall be established forever, but a lying tongue is a but for a moment." (Proverbs 12:19)
-It is written.

10th commandment

"You shall not **covet** your neighbor's house, you shall not covet your neighbor's wife, nor his male servant, nor his female servant, nor his ox, nor his donkey, nor anything that is your neighbor's." (Exodus 20:17)

You shall not **covet**. Covet is from the Hebrew word **chamad**. It means; To delight in beauty, greatly beloved, covet, delectable thing, delight, desire, <u>lust,</u> (be) pleasant, precious.

Here we can see that covet from the Hebrew language means several things. One of the words is **Lust**. The meaning of the word lust is; A strong feeling of sexual desire.

It is written

"Jesus Christ is the same yesterday, today, and forever." (Hebrews 13:8)

Notes;

_____

_____

_____

_____

_____

60

Notes;

CHAPTER 7

Sin

Sin - Humans love it

They love to follow their' feelings.' The thoughts that come from Satan, they come so comfortable that man loves to obey them right away. They love to follow their thoughts and their feelings. They love sin, which made them love to do it.
They love to feel that they have control.

But the Lord tells us to seek His Kingdom first

"But seek first the kingdom of God and His righteousness, and all these things shall be added to you." (Matthew 6:33)

We have a God who wants to have a community with us. He wants to give us His Holy Spirit. He wants to teach us all the things that we need to know. He is the one that loves us so much, amidst our flaws to the point where He gave His only be-gotten son for all of us. (John 3:16)

The Lord loves to do miracles, and He loves to have a relationship with His children.

Yet we chose to sin, and we decide to walk in our ways, yet we reject the living God. We love to satisfy our fleshly desires, as we like to think that we are right.

-We kick the Holy Ghost out. **What a tragedy**.

We profess Jesus with our lips, but deny Him with our deeds. (Titus 1:16)

There is absolutely no difference
Someone is sitting in a pub. He is not saved but is sitting there and pouring in. It is, of course, ladies at this pub, and he who eagerly pouring in, he has his thoughts when it becomes to these ladies. The more beer that is being ingested, the more beautiful these women will be.

Let us see what the Scripture says about those who are pouring in alcohol and commit adultery with their eyes.

The Bible says this about alcohol
"Wine is a mocker, strong drink is a brawler. And whoever is led astray by it is not wise." (Proverbs 20:1)

The Bible says about those who commit adultery
"But I say to you that whoever looks at a woman to lust for her has already committed adultery with her in his heart." (Matthew 5:28)

Let us read the Lord's 7th Commandment;
"You shall not commit adultery." (Exodus 20:14)

He who sits on the pub and pours alcohol in, and looks at these females with lust, is guilty of adultery in Gods' eyes.

But in 'church' one Sunday;
Sits two persons on row 13. One of them is in the leadership, and the other is a prayer leader. It is half an hour before the church service starts. They choose to backbite and to be rebellious against the Lord our God.
Being rebellious means; would not stoop - discard the word of God.

This is something that most people like non-believers as believers. Namely that it floats the venom out of our mouths, about someone that is not present. To listen to backbiting is the same as you participate in it.

Let's see what scripture says about rebellion and backbiting.

The Bible says
"For rebellion is as the sin of witchcraft. And stubbornness is as iniquity and idolatry. Because you have rejected the word of the Lord, He also has rejected you from being king."
(1 Samuel 15:23)

Katalalia, the Hebrew word for **backbiting**, which means; Evil speaking.

Backbiting is a rebellion against God.

64

"For by your words you will be justified, and by your words, you will be condemned." (Matthew 12:37)

Warnings against backbiting
The Bible is evident in this field. Backbiting is something that is forbidden.
Any backbiting is a sin. Backbiting is like sweet candy, we can say that we do not like it, but when it's within our reach, we just can't resist it. We get a sudden appetite for knowing what we do not know about others - either negative or positive.

Why is it so hard to quit?
Proverbs 18:8 says, "The words of a talebearer are like tasty trifles, and they go down into the inmost body."

No, you might think, not me.
I'm not taking part in slandering other people this way.
-Gossip comes in many varieties, and it also involves listening.

Proverbs 17:4 says: "An evildoer gives heed to false lips, a liar listens eagerly to a spiteful tongue."

"Do not speak evil of one another, brethren. He who speaks evil of a brother and judges his brother, speaks evil of the law and judges the law." (James 4:11)

"Therefore, laying aside all malice, all deceit, hypocrisy, envy, and all evil speaking." (1 Peter 2:1)

The wrath of God to the injustice

"For the wrath of God is revealed from heaven against all un-godliness and unrighteousness of men, who suppress the truth in unrighteousness." (Romans 1:18)

"But those things which proceed out of the mouth come from the heart, and they defile a man. For out of the heart proceed evil thoughts, murders, adulteries, fornications, thefts, false witness, **blasphemies**." (Matthew 15:18-19)

Blasphemia is a Greek word, and it means **evil speaking**.

Is there any difference between the one who is pouring in at the pub and those who sit in the congregation and backbite?
No, for the Lord, it is in the same category called sin.

To the most important

Who will preach about the repentance from sin for those who are mentioned here? Who will enter the dark pub and use the boldness that he has received from the Lord? Who shall use their boldness to preach repentance from sin to those backbiting 'leaders' in the congregation?

Is it the evangelist? Or is it the 'pastor'?

The evangelist cannot preach inside the church because there are the 'pastor' and the leadership kings.

The 'pastor' is a way to 'holy' to go to the pub. Most probably he will warn us to go to the pub. This is how it is today.

This kind of attitude is so far away from the Lord's will as there is to come.

All of us shall preach the message of repentance
The question is to whom? The answer is: to everyone who needs it.

In Matthew 9:12, we read the word sick. Sick is from the Greek word **Kakos**. It means; Badly (physically or morally) amiss, diseased, **evil**, grievously, miserably, sick, sore.

Now you've got a Biblical understanding of how Jesus did it. -Go and do the same.

"Most assuredly, I say to you, he who believes in Me, the works that I do he will do also, and greater works than these he will do, because I go to My Father." (John 14:12)

If you believe and have laid down your life for Christ, you will do the same as Christ did. (Mark 16:15)

For the wages of sin is death
Humanity was created to live his life in and with God, who is the source of life. But the unhappily happened, man breaking free from this life in unity with the Creator. They sinned by his disobedience to God's commandment.
-There is only one wage of sin; Death.

"For the wages of sin is death, but the gift of God is eternal life in Christ Jesus our Lord." (Romans 6:23)

"Then, when desire has conceived, it gives birth to sin, and sin, when it is full-grown, brings forth death." (James 1:15)

Do not be deceived the Bible says
"Jesus answered and said to them, you are mistaken, not knowing the Scriptures nor the power of God." (Matthew 22:29)

Death is the wrath of God's judgment over sin.

One of Satan's name is the tempter
"Now when the tempter came to him, he said, if you are the Son of God, command that these stones become bread." (Matthew 4:3)

How sin gets a hitch
We live in a world full of temptations. In all sin, there are pleasures and temptations within. Let us see what is written in James 1:15. "Then, when desire has conceived, it gives birth to sin, and sin, when it is full-grown, brings forth death!"

What is sin?
All that contradicts the Word of God is a sin.

A little thought gives birth to the most significant sin
It all begins with a little thought. You begin to satisfy this thought, and it grows a bit more, now you begin to accept the next thought that has the same lousy content. (Just a little bit different)
These thoughts become nursed.

When that is done, you are ready to perform the sin, whatever it might be that goes against God's Word.

Man, tend to trusts his emotions.
God has given us weapons against this. Discerning between spirits. Discern what is from Satan and the demons, or what is from the Holy Spirit.

The leaven of the Pharisees, the same as today's leaven in many congregations
When you have a dough with yeast in, one thinks a tiny portion of yeast and a more significant piece of dough.

The baker wants to have more yeast to speed up the raising.
A given time passes, and the dough is a finished product. But if you think a little bit different, it needs only a little bit yeast in the dough, and then it is only the time it stands on until every-thing is permeated.

A leader in a church that has leaven in his teaching
Time passes, and all that takes after this leader becomes imbued by his leaven.

Therefore, all Christians must go out in the world (among the heathen) and be trained by the Holy Spirit.
-This is crucial for you to become a mature Christian.

"Till we all come to the unity of the faith, and of the knowledge of the Son of God, to a perfect man, to the measure of the stature of the fullness of Christ." (Ephesians 4:13)

Why is this necessary?
"That we should no longer be children, tossed to and fro and carried about with every wind of doctrine, by the trickery of men, in the cunning craftiness of deceitful plotting."
(Ephesians 4:14)

When you speak the truth, you'll speak the truth
If what you speak contains untruths, then it is all an untruth.

How often it is the 'truth' that is preached, but suddenly something shows up that is not according to Scripture.
We as Christians, very easy 'accepts' a preacher who we follow, or use some of the material to learn. We tend to swallow everything because he is a 'popular' preacher.

Leaven is through the scripture, used as an image of impurity, wickedness, and hypocrisy.

Let's take a look at four different kinds of leaven;

Legalism
"A little leaven leavens the whole lump." (Galatians 5:9)

Wickedness
"Therefore let us keep the feast, not with old leaven, nor with the leaven of malice and wickedness, but with the unleavened bread of sincerity and truth." (1 Corinthians 5:8)

False Teachings

"How is it you do not understand that I did not speak to you concerning bread? But beware of the leaven of the Pharisees and Sadducees. Then they understood that He did not tell them to beware of the leaven of bread, but of the doctrine of the Pharisees and Sadducees." (Matthew 16:11-12)

Hypocrisy

"In the meantime, when an innumerable multitude of people had gathered together so that they trampled one another, He began to say to His disciples, first of all, be aware of the leaven of the Pharisees, which is hypocrisy." (Luke 12:1)

What Jesus warns to us is evilness in which - if it comes into the church, spreading out and growing, so that it eventually permeates the whole lump. (Romans 12:1-2)

Try the spirits

Sad to say, not many can tell how to discern between spirits. We all are function in it, but we need to be able to understand it.

There exist a misunderstanding regarding the distinguishing of the Spirits. Now, I shall not go into the gifts of the Spirit in 1 Corinthians 12, but to the book of Hebrews.

The Bible says

"For everyone who partakes only of milk is unskilled in the word of righteousness, for he is a babe. But solid food belongs to those who are of full age, that is, those who by reason of use

have their senses exercised to discern both good and evil."
(Hebrews 5:13-14)

We can see here that to discern between the good and the evil, is something that we must exert our senses in.
This applies to all Christians.

We read the word, **discern** in verse 14. Discern is from the Greek word **diakrisis**. It means; Discern.
Diakrisis - discern, is the same word that is used in 1 Corinthians 12:10, regarding the discerning of spirits.

All spirits must be tried. Who shall try the spirits? All Christians.

Are you still someone who needs to run after someone else to learn? Are you one who has not entered the fullness of Christ? Then it is not about 'if' you have the gift or not, but that you still are drinking milk like a helpless baby.

Not to get into the fullness of Christ, the Bible warns against.

The Bible says
"That we should no longer be children, tossed to and fro and carried about with every wind of doctrine, by the trickery of men, in the cunning craftiness of deceitful plotting."
(Ephesians 4:14)

In verse 14, we read the word **children**. Children are from the Greek word **nepios**.

It means: Not speaking, i.e., an infant (minor), a simple-minded person, <u>an immature Christian</u>, babe, child (ish).

In these cases, it is essential to relate to what scripture says, nothing else.

It is many of the 'big' popular preachers who have written dozens of books. Many of these books are sold in millions of copies to Christians worldwide. One day, for example, you see several of them have been in an audience with the pope. After this, there come statements that are not according to Scripture.

In short;
If their teaching contains any untruth, then everything is an untruth. You may interpret it in the flesh and will say: But he has so much great to say, how can everything be false?

It does not matter what people think or feel: the only thing that matters is what the Bible says.

If the Bible says; If there is any leaven, the <u>whole</u> lump is sour.

Love not the world
"Do not love the world or the things in the world. If anyone loves the world, the love of the Father is not in him."
(1 John 2:15)

All sin must come to an end in your life
It is not okay to have any sin in your life. If you have such, you have opened the door for Satan. Thus, he has the right to torment you. Think about it.

If we as believers expect a life of spiritual authority, a life wherein the Lord elevates us up in spiritual understanding, then all sin must come to an end and be repented from.

We are freed from sin and born to a life of Christ
We are freed from sin. We should no longer live by the lust of the flesh. The Bible says if we live after the flesh, we shall die. But if by the Spirit kill the deeds of the body, you shall live.

"For to be <u>carnally</u> minded is death, but to be <u>spiritually</u> minded is life and peace." (Romans 8:6)

When we live in the lust of the flesh, then we are not pleasing God. We are and will be a discomfort for the Lord when we live in the flesh. This is a severe matter.
Compliance with the lust of the flesh is completely forbidden for a person who is born again.

"So then, those who are in the flesh cannot please God." (Romans 8:8)

We do not owe the flesh anything. Therefore we do not need to live according to the lust of the flesh.

They want freedom, but what kind of freedom?
Every summer, there is a gay pride parade in our city. I read on their website that a lot of their work is to tell and show others how to live a life as gay and 'free.' Free to do precisely what they want.

What they want is to go against God's written Word and His will in the Bible. It is a sin and sin alone who is Lord in these assemblies.
-No God they are interested in.

Prince of this world is their master
The prince of this world is the one who became a master when you have this attitude to 'freedom.'

"Whose minds the god of this age has blinded, who do not believe, lest the light of the gospel of the glory of Christ, who is the image of God, should shine on them." (2 Corinthians 4:4)

God will not hear the sinners
"If I regard iniquity in my heart, the Lord will not hear."
(Psalm 66:18)

"Now we know that God does not hear sinners, but if anyone is a worshiper of God and does His will, He hears him."
(John 9:31)

"The Lord is far from the wicked, but He hears the prayer of the righteous." (Proverbs 15:29)

"Now this is the confidence that we have in Him, that if we ask anything according to His will, He hears us." (1 John 5:14)

Shout from your heart: Jesus! Forgive me; I have sinned. **Only then, He will hear**.

"If we confess our sins, He is faithful and just to forgive us our sins and to cleanse us from all unrighteousness." (1 John 1:9)

Notes;

_____

_____

_____

_____

_____

_____

_____

_____

76

Notes;

CHAPTER 8

Demons

Demons. It can be said a lot about this subject. We will look at some of the basics.

Demons are intelligent, they can communicate, and they speak different languages.

We let the scripture tell
"And when He had come out of the boat, **immediately** there met Him out of the tombs a man with an unclean spirit, who had his dwelling among the tombs, and no one could bind him, not even with chains, because he had often been bound with shackles and chains. And the chains had been pulled apart by him, and the shackles broken in pieces, neither could anyone tame him. And always, night and day, he was in the mountains and in the tombs, crying out and cutting himself with stones. **When he saw Jesus from afar**, he ran and worshipped Him. And he cried out with a loud voice and said; what have I to do with You, Jesus, Son of the most high God? I implore You by God that You do not torment me." (Mark 5:2-7)

We shall live in daily victory over Satan and the demons, and not have any focus on all the bad experiences that they come up with. The demons only want your attention to control you. To have control over you to make sure you'll fall.

Fall and fail in every part of your journey with the Lord. They want to destroy all the revelations, and they want to destroy you, kill you, and steal everything from you. That's the promise in John 10:10.

All this they work with 24/7.

The thief does not come except to steal, and to kill, and to destroy. (John 10:10)

The Bible tells us how we should relate to this

"Behold, I give you the authority to trample on serpents and scorpions, and over all the power of the enemy, and nothing shall by any means hurt you." (Luke 10:19)

Jesus must be our main focus

"Nevertheless do not rejoice in this, that the spirits are subject to you, but rather rejoice because your names are written in heaven." (Luke 10:20)

The Spirit of Self-Pity

You might feel that you are badly treated by the people around you. Perhaps, you have been badly treated in social media. There might have been some disagreements between you and your family or in your community. Or maybe you live abroad, and just miss your family.

Every time this demon is showing up, he tends to use different strategies to reach you. No matter what happens, Satan will invade your thoughts, and blame you for how bad you have been to the other person(s).

Other times, he reverses his strategy and displaying how bad others have been to you, and how many good things you have done to these people.

Then comes the bomb. Self-pity descends on you, and you feel almost anxiety and dissatisfaction.

It might come to a few tears while you are feeling sorry for yourself.

If you agree to these self-pity thoughts, then you agree to a demon with the same name. You take those thoughts that he cometh with, thinking that they are entirely in it's a 'proper' place.

It is now which you have taken a demon in your arms and started to cuddle with it. Everything that this demon has come with, you think is 'right.'

This demon is easy to recognize; You feel self-pity.

If you are not able to try the spirits, then you will be an easy target for this demon.

The way I have described this is how I dealt with these kinds of spiritual powers. The times of which I have been exposed, I feel in my body that the spirit comes. Immediately it is told to leave in Jesus' Name.

The thoughts this spirit comes with, I do not entertain one single second.

Nor do we find in scripture that a demon comes alone, or operates only in one task. Comes there a demon, and I expose it, I have my whole guard up for what he starts to blame me for.

Spirit of self-pity is a demon of death and destruction.
-A demon that has managed to kill hundreds of thousands of people.

Your thought life is Satan's arena

Come into a position with your life where you have spiritual understanding.
If you understand, you will reveal demons. Can you reveal them, you have the authority. No revealing, no authority.
You have no authority cause you do not know what is going on.

Demons = Control

A generic term for all demons is that all of them operate in/under control to gain domination through manipulation.
What they tempt you with, they do just to gain control over you.
And when you take it, when you allow temptations to come, then you will be caught in their spider web of control.
This comes in many different ways from the enemy.

Discussions - an area where demons are right around the corner

The garden party is right around the corner. Everything has been made perfect for this weekend among good friends.
Everybody comes with expectations.

-Everything runs smoothly, and the food is excellent; wines and champagne bottles are opened. Discussions about small and greater things are about to come.

-Then it explodes! Anger has been able to enter some of the guests. Unsettled actions from the past became a topic suddenly. Demons come up with knowledge from the past. They have been waiting for the 'door' to be opened for them.

Demons love this setting in immature believers or the unsaved. They act only on what is written in John 10:10. Nothing else they are interested in.

When unsettled matters occur from the past, and we agree with it, the distance to anger and forgiveness is short.

If you do not understand how the demons are working, you will lose. Why? Because you do not discern the spirits and you, do not live according to God's written word.

Did Jesus say that it is ok to be angry?
"Be angry, and <u>do not sin</u>, do not let the sun go down on your wrath." (Ephesians 4:26)

If you go against this scripture, you give Satan approved access.

"Nor give place to the devil." (Ephesians 4:27)

Did Jesus say it is ok to obey a temptation spirit that comes with knowledge from the past?

You do not discern between good and evil because you haven't exercised your senses. (Hebrews 5:14)

Christians need to pull themselves together and enter into a spiritual understanding of things.

The Bible says that those who live by the flesh shall not inherit the kingdom of God. (Galatians 5:19-21)
Therefore the Bible says that we shall not trust our feelings. If we live by the scripture, God will show you things through your feelings, but you can only trust (discern right) them if they are according to the Scriptures.
There is only one thing to say; The Bible, read and meditate on it day and night. (Joshua 1:8) And be a doer of the word. (James 1:22)

"The fear of the Lord is to hate evil; Pride and arrogance and the evil way And the perverse mouth I hate." (Proverbs 8:13)

Believers should live a Holy life and shall not imitate the world
"I beseech you, therefore, brethren, by the mercies of God, that you present your bodies a living sacrifice, holy, acceptable to God, which is your reasonable service. And do not be conformed to this world, but be transformed by the renewing of your mind, that you may prove what is that good and acceptable and perfect will of God." (Romans 12:1-2)

How can a Holy Ghost teach you all things (John 14:26) when you are not willing to obey Christ's commandments?
(Luke 6:46)

They are everywhere
You must enter a position with your life, where you distinguish between spirits.
-This is the most crucial matter in your Christian life. If not, you are unable to discern between Satan, the demons, and the Holy Ghost. This is being deceived.

Do not think if you have that gift or not.
-All Christians shall discern between spirits.

We read one more time in the book of Hebrews;
"But solid food belongs to those who are of full age, that is, those who by reason of use have their senses exercised to discern both good and evil." (Hebrews 5:14)

A Christian life without daily active discerning between spirits is not a life in victory, but living in disobedient and misery.

They come into your dreams
You lie in your bed at peace, closing your eyes for the night. Then the cowards (demons) shows up to put fear in you. The nightmares suddenly appear. It comes to you when you are in your sleep. All the demons want is to put fear in you, enough of it for you to remember the next days.
In this matter, you must trust the Lord that He is with you.

"Assuredly, I say to you, whatever you bind on earth will be bound in heaven, and whatever you loose on earth will be loosed in heaven." (Matthew 18:18)

Maybe they have tied you up. Perhaps it has been snakes that have bitten you. There are absolutely no limits to what this evilness can do.

Nothing is more important to understand what the Bible says about spiritual warfare.
The warfare, in which you are a part of 365 days a year.

There is no doubt that these kinds of attacks are sometimes heavy to live by.
But it is Jesus that we belong to, and we have been given the power to trample on snakes and scorpions. (Luke 10:19)
What visits you in your dreams has only one intention, and that is to destroy. (John 10:10)

Will God speak through your dreams? Yes, He will. But again, discernment is what brings you into an understanding of who the author of the dreams is.

I remember many episodes of similar attacks in my life. It was especially in times where I believed the Lord for new things of spiritual matters in my ministry. But it is God's written word I rely on, nothing else.

In these matters, we have to show Satan and the demons which we are in Christ.

Temptation spirits

You sit down and read your Bible, and then something starts to happen. A temptation spirit comes sneaking. You notice it, but you do not take it seriously.

You think you have control over the situation, and continue the reading as nothing has happened.

You do not take it seriously because you do not live after the scripture that says in this matter; "bring every thought into captivity to the obedience of Christ." (2 Corinthians 10:5)

What these demons come with under your Bible reading are temptations to distract you and cease you from reading.

After some thousand-odd years of practice, they always come sneaking. You begin to accept a little thought, seconds later, you check your mobile phone, or you stop reading entirely.

You became tempted, started to entertain the temptation thought. This is like throwing gasoline on the fire.

"Blessed is the man who endures temptation; for when he has been approved, he will receive the crown of life which the Lord has promised to those who love Him." (James 1:12)

Temptations come in all kinds of varieties and sizes. We must capture them all under the obedience of Christ.

Python spirit

You probably noticed it, maybe more times than you realize.

-For example, one Sunday, you are on the way to church. Last night's sleep was excellent, and you are having such a great day. On-time, the church starts. Maybe it starts with 3-4 worship songs, and then some testimonies followed.
Everything runs on tracks, and people are moved.
The pastor begins to preach the word of God, and then it starts to happen.

-You begin to feel a little bit tired, maybe a small yawn shows up, mixed with a small dosage of distraction.
You do not react so much to it. The chance that a python spirit is on the move now is significant.

A python spirit is a strangling spirit.
It doesn't strangle you right away, but it gently starts to choke you. When you accept this tiredness, the python spirit will continue his 'squeezing' work.
The disaster is soon a fact, and you were not able to grasp the content - revelation of today's teaching.
You left home glad and positive, and now you are suddenly tired and out of focus.

A python spirit is a very astute spirit. But are you willing to learn, it is simple to enter an understanding of how it is working. When you reveal it, it has no authority.

Neither Satan nor the demons have nothing against the word of God. But they are terrified that you will be the mighty giant the Lord has called you to be.

The Bible says;
"Therefore submit to God. Resist the devil and he will flee from you." (James 4:7)

When the Holy Ghost, who is the spirit of revelation, (John 14:26) begins to reveal the word for you; When you start to act on the written word of Almighty God, Satan and the demons will come after you. (Ephesians 6:12)

Satan will not accept that you start to grow in the word of God. He does not accept that you begin to pray for the sick, and he definitely will not accept that you start to cast out demons.
-But how much shall you accept from Satan? **Nothing**.

We stand on the word of God.
We have been given authority to trample on serpents and scorpions, and all the powers of the enemy. (Luke 10:19)
-Now we must learn to use the authority.

Does the Bible say anything about python spirits?
Yes, it does.

The Bible says in Acts 16:16 about a slave girl that was possessed with a spirit of divination.

Let us read from verse 16-18.
"Now it happened, as we went to prayer, that a certain slave girl possessed with a spirit of **divination** met us, who brought her masters much profit by fortune-telling. This girl followed Paul and us, and cried out, saying, **these men are the servants of the**

Most High God, who proclaim to us the way of salvation.
And this she did for many days. But Paul, greatly annoyed,
turned and said to the spirit, I command you in the name of Jesus Christ to come out of her. And he came out that very hour."

We see that the girl had a spirit of divination, who could predict.
It was able to tell others upfront who the Apostles were, and that
they were going to preach the message of salvation to the sinners.
We can see that the demon does not have anything against God's
written word and His work.
This slave girl followed the disciples for several days, only for
destroying their works of the Lord.

"The thief (Satan) does not come except to steal, and to kill, and
to destroy." (John 10:10)

**"I (Jesus) have come that they may have life and that they
may have it more abundantly."** (John 10:10)

The slave girl prophesied - predicted over the disciples, and
have then spiritual revelation about it.

Let us read Acts 16:16 in the King James version;
"And it came to pass, as we went to prayer, a certain **damsel
possessed** with a spirit of **divination** met us, which brought her
masters much gain by soothsaying." (Acts 16:16)

Damsel means woman. **Possessed**, means from the Greek language: possessed with, accompany.

Spirit of divination means; **Python**.

She was possessed with a python spirit that is also was able to predict.

One of the areas that a python spirit is working in is fortune-telling. This is; Prophetic and horoscope. And horoscope is in the 'occult.' No matter where you move in the occult, you will encounter a python spirit. There is also no warranty from scripture that this spirit works alone.

The prophetic through other believers and the church

Many are prophesizing to the left and the right. It is only one way to find out what is prophesied over/to you is correct.
-You must discern the spirits.

The purpose of the horoscope is: increase insight into a person's character and talk about the future.
-Have you fallen into the temptation to read or receive this week's horoscope through a Newspaper or online services?
If so, the chance is significant that a python spirit has gotten a hold of you. Repentance to the Lord is what you must do.
So easy it is; So severe it becomes.

The Bible says;

"Try the spirits if, whether they are of God." (1 John 4:1)

"God forbids any divination." (Deuteronomy 18:10, 14)

"Our trust is in Christ alone." (Hebrews 12:2)

When you sin, you open the door to the spiritual. Then comes spirits, and they are demons.

If we mess with wrong spiritual things, wrong spirits are coming. You have opened the door because you have gone against God's written word.

If the Lord says, you shall not seek/receive horoscope. And you said, it is only a magazine that I had bought.

Then you have gone in agreement with Satan, and he is now allowed by you to torment you. Neither Satan or the demons leave before you have surrendered to the Lord and repents your sins.

"Come to Me, all you who labor and are heavy laden, and I will give you rest." (Matthew 11:28)

"And you shall know the truth, and the truth shall make you free." (John 8:32)

It is a victory, do not be defeated by proud infidel acts.

Notes;

_____

_____

_____

_____

CHAPTER 9

Signs and Wonders follow

On my way home

It's been another fabulous day with the Lord, and a good friend of mine. Out there, bringing the Gospel to the sick and the broken-hearted. We preached all over the town this day, and many were healed.

We were standing on a road cross, waiting for the green light. Suddenly a taxi stopped in the middle of the street, and shouted out of the window: Hey, can you guys come to my place? I have someone in my house that needs healing.

I thank God for our banners that we are carrying every time we are out on the streets.
Countless times, people have seen them from a distance and rushed over to us for their needs.
4-5 hours later this day, it was time for us to go home.
This day, like many other days when we decide to end preaching, the Lord has other plans.

I stopped at a local bakery shop to buy some Coca-Cola.
-Two cans of coke please, I said to the woman behind the counter. She looked strangely at me and did not respond to my

order. Suddenly she started to talk rapidly to the others who were working there, in their local language that I do not understand much of.

-Now she pointed at me and said: You are the guy that walks around with that big banner.

Yes, that is right, I answered. What can I do for you?

-I have arthritis and pain all over my body, she said with a sad face.

"Go over to the side of the counter, and I will pray for you," I replied.

I started to pray, and you could see right away that the Lord was moving.

All the customers at the bakery were witnessing what was happening at the end of the counter.

-When the cashier lady had her prayer, I asked everyone in the line if they needed healing. And indeed, there was. Ten minutes later, seven people have been healed from various pains and sicknesses.

-I paid for the coke and went home.

New ankle

It was Saturday and town day in the little town of Carmen.

We had decided to go there to preach the Gospel and to heal the sick. It attends a few thousand people once a week on this day in Carmen. They come to buy and sell or just looking.

We were ten people in our team this day, which witnessed and preached throughout the day.

People got their hearing back; countless back problems were healed; kidneys restored, and others got new body parts.
-110 people were healed this day, and much more had heard the Gospel of Jesus Christ.

People gathered around us in a big circle.
-It was then I made a huge mistake, but God in His greatness turned it into His glory.

Suddenly, I saw him - the man with the crutches.
-Hello, I said, what is wrong with your leg, and if you want, I can pray for you?
It was a lot of noise there, so I did not hear all that he has answered.

-I heard something about the ankle, and since it was many people to pray for, I did not waste my time.
I bent down, laid my hand on his ankle, and commanded arthritis to go away in Jesus' name.

-That turned out to be the mistake of the day. Because while I am praying, he said to me that it is not arthritis, that is the problem.
-I could not do anything else than to smile.
What is wrong, then I asked?
He smiled and said that he had been involved in a motorcycle accident five years ago, where his ankle got crushed.
After the accident, I was in bed for a year with my leg lifted high before I could start walking with crutches, he said.
-Did you not go to a hospital after the accident?

No, I did not have money for that, he replied.

In the western part of the world where I live, we run to the pharmacy if we cough a little bit. And now I am standing in front of someone who had the ankle crushed, and had laid in bed for a whole year so the ankle could be stiff enough so he could walk on it.

-It is only one thing to do, I said to him. "We must pray to Jesus."
I prayed to the Lord for a new ankle.
Right after the short prayer, I told him to start moving the ankle around.
-How are you now, I said?
Slowly, he started to move the ankle around and around.
-A few minutes later, he walked away with his crutches on his shoulder.
He was healed.

What a powerful God we have.
If I can do this, so can you.

Alice
A preschool teacher from the little suburb of Booy. She is a Catholic and therefore needs everything that has to do with Jesus. Her school is not like any other school, and this one is in between the many other houses where people live.
-I have been in that area many times and ministered to people living there. I have friends that have kids in this school, that's

one of the reasons the door was opened to give Alice the true
Gospel of Jesus Christ.

One time that I came to her school, and I guess she was not ex-
pecting at all what would happen.
While I stood there in the door opening and talked to her, one of
the neighbors called me. I said excuse for a while to Alice and
went down there to see what was going on. It was the father of
one of the kids that I have prayed for earlier, who got healed
from arthritis.

-What is going on? I said to him.
Can you please pray for that boy over there, and pointed at the
end of the garden.
-I went down there with him, and in a bed made of bamboo lays
a 15-16-year-old kid writhing in pain.
What is the problem? I asked the boy.
-It is the stomach he answered.
The man who has called me said he was scheduled for the hospi-
tal later this day.
-Can you please pray for him, the people standing around this
boy said.

"Just a minute," I answered and started to walk up to the
preschool. I knocked on Alice's door and asked if she could
come with me for I would show her something.
-Ok, she said, and we walked over to the sick boy.
Do you see this boy with this pain? I asked Alice. "Yes," she
said with a sad face.

-Lay your hands on his stomach, and tell the pain to go I said to her.

"No, I cannot!" she replied.

-Yes, you can. Lay your hands on his stomach and command the pain to go in Jesus' Name.

"Okay," she said, and started to pray.

-When she was finished, I told the boy to stand up.

How do you feel now I asked him.

-He checked frantically on the stomach to see if he could find the pain.

Do you see what just happened? I asked Alice.

"Yes, I see," she answered.

-The boy was healed, and he does not need to go to the hospital now.

She walked back to the preschool, shocked by what just happened.

Healed through the window

After a long day of preaching the Gospel, it was nice to come home.

My banner was parked as usual under the stair. I was looking forward to some rest.

-But my wife had other plans.

She pleased me to go to the mall for some shopping.

-This I was not at all interested in, but family matters are also important.

After the mall, she wanted to make a quick stop at the local flower market.

-Now, I was not very positive anymore, but I let myself be persuaded.

The flower market is in an open field and is not inside a building. Then, I could stay in the car while she was looking at orchids.

While I sat there, I saw someone on the other side of the street that I have ministered to before.

-Hey, how are you? I shouted out of the car window.

Not so good, she replied.

-Come over here and tell me what is wrong!

I have significant pain in my back, she said.

-Do you want me to pray for you? I asked.

Yes, please.

I was still inside of the car, so I stretched my hand out of the window, and laid it on her back and commanded it to be healed in Jesus' name.

-How do you feel now?

She just smiled from one ear to another. Healed.

While I prayed for her, some other people were walking on the other side of the road, and you could see that they were curious about what was happening.

-They came over and started to ask a lot of questions to the woman who just got healed.

"I was healed," she said.

-How much does it cost? They asked me.

-Nothing I said.

Suddenly, the whole atmosphere changed. Now people started to gather around the car.

There was something wrong with all of them, and one by one, the Lord healed all of them.

The last person was timid, so I had to go out of the car to pray for her.

When my wife came back with the new flowers, I was just sitting there and smiling.

-So many times, when we want to give up for the day, the Lord has other plans.

The bus driver and the healing cloth

Usually, we eat lunch at the local bakery at City Square, when we are evangelizing along the busy streets of Tagbilaran City. Outside this bakery, there is a small bus terminal, and on a few couples of occasions, I have preached to the bus drivers there. Especially one of the drivers got my attention.

-He looked like a nice guy, but there was no doubt that there was a heavy burden on his shoulders.

Sorry, I said to my lunch mates, I have to talk to the man over there.

-Hello, I said to the bus driver, "How are you?

I am ok, but my wife is not, he responded.

-What is wrong with your wife I asked him.

It is her neck and her shoulders. She has been to several doctors, but she is not getting any better! Can you come to my place and pray for her?

-Where do you live, I replied?

One hour with the car from here, he said.

-It is a little bit far to go for me just to pray for one person I told him.

In the Philippines, very few can afford to go to a hospital or doctor when something is wrong. In most cases, they stay at home and hope that the pain or sickness shall leave them.

-I told the bus driver that I could give him a healing cloth, and when he comes home, he just has to follow the instructions written on the paper that was together with the piece of garment.

Okay, he said, I will do that.

-He seems like he was not convinced, but he put the cloth in the glove department on the bus.

One month later, my wife and I were on the way home from town, and then I spotted the bus driver who he was relaxing in a parking place. I turned in and parked in front of his bus.

-Hello there, how are you, my friend?

I am very okay. When I came home after the last time we talked, I did as you told me to do. I laid the cloth on my wife's back and a couple of other places on her body.

-And then what happened? I asked him.

All the pain left her body! Was it a magic cloth you gave me?

No, my friend. It was not magic in that cloth. It was the real deal, and His name is Jesus Christ, our Lord, and Savior!

He who took all the sins of the world on Him and by His stripes, we have been healed.

-No magic here, my friend, I told him with a big smile on my face.

We rejoiced and thanked the Lord for the miracle.

The cake

We were on the way to the beach for baptizing some brothers and sisters, and to celebrate a birthday.

Late, as usual, we struggled through the morning traffic.

-The birthday cake had to be picked up in the middle of town before we could head-on for the beach.

I parked outside the main entrance of the mall, and my wife went in to get the birthday cake.

The clock was ticking. When you park in the middle of the road, it's like time is standing still. Next to the car, 8-10 people sat with their sales both. Some were repairing shoes, and others were selling flowers.

-While I was sitting there, a thought comes to me; "you have time."

-I jumped out of the car and asked the lady at the first booth if she had any pain that she needed healing from.

She hesitated to answer.

-I asked the same question again, and this time I said: If you have any pain or sickness, remember that Jesus Christ has been whipped for you to be healed.

I have shoulder pain, she said. I laid my hand on her shoulder and commanded it to be healed in Jesus' name.

I asked her right after I prayed how she feels.

-No pain was the answer.

Healed! Thank you, Lord.

Okay, in the next booth sat a gentleman that just had witnessed what happened to the lady, so no more in-depth explanation was needed.

-He just got a simple question if he needed healing.

"Yes," he said, I have pain all over my body.

-Be more specific, I told him.

"My shoulder," he said.

-I commanded the shoulder to be healed in Jesus' name. And then I asked him where the pain was.

All the pain was gone is the answer.

-Healed.

This happened in the middle of an intersection.

Jesus is fantastic when we believe and act upon His written word.

The printing store

When you are evangelizing in the streets, equipment of different kinds is something that you need for the work.

T-shirts with diverse print on are something that works very well. Places where our banners are not fitting, t-shirts do the work. This day, I was in the printing store to make some new ones. And while you are sitting there and waiting, you can choose either to just sit there and wait, or you can look for an opening to preach the Gospel.

-I waited for an opportunity to bring the Glory of the Lord to someone.

It was evident that the person who did my t-shirts, who is also is the owner of the store, had a severe neck problem.

-I asked her what was wrong with her neck, but she said: Nothing.

-There is something wrong I said, "you are stiff!"

I stood up and walked over to the back of the counter.

-I laid my hand on her neck and commanded the pain to go in Jesus' name.

She jumped in the chair halfway in my prayer.

What did you do? And she looked frantic after the pain.

-You will not find the pain I said to her because Jesus has healed you.

I paid for the t-shirts, she got healed, and the name of Christ was lifted. Glory.

Lady with a cane

CPG Avenue, the main street of Tagbilaran City.

This bustling street was a place that I always walked by with my banner. And one day, outside a bank, an older woman with a cane stood with her grandchild.

-I stopped and asked if what was wrong with her.

Arthritis, I had it for 12-15 years, and it is terrible, she answered.

This type of sickness is an incurable disease seen from the medicine's side and can be kept only in check with medications. Satan got what he wanted. First, he bounded this lady with the disease, and then he bound her to be a forever customer at hospitals and pharmacies.

-I started to preach about the crucified Christ, and by his stripes, she had been healed.

After little preaching, I asked if I could pray for her.

-She said, "yes," then I gave arthritis a short commandment to leave her body right away.

She just looked strange at me.

-I told her to lay down the cane and start moving around.

Step by step, she gently started to walk around. She just looked at me with her one hand covering her mouth.

Your cane, you do not need it anymore because the Lord has healed you, I said.

Every time I experience this, my heart is pounding with joy.

-The older woman was healed.

Now she wanted my phone number, for many in her town was sick and needed healing.

-Thank you, Lord.

A Friday

Downtown the day before, I had prayed for a lady who got healed from some back issues.

She asked me if I could come to the area where she lived because it was many there who were sick.

-I had said yes to this, and now I was there with a small team of 4 people.

She lived near a fruit market and a bus terminal.

This day, it rained and rained, and it was a big blessing that this area was under a roof.

Spiritually, this area is heavy to evangelize in. But we focus on the commandments of Christ and not to the circumstances. It started with people who got healed from knee pain, headaches, back pain, and so on.

-It was just amazing to see how the Holy Ghost moved in people.

Four hours later, all of us were very tired. But God Almighty does not let Satan win.

-This day, more than 50 people got healed.
More than 50 people saw the living God in action.

Are you one who walk with the Holy Ghost power, people will see the light in you. (Matthew 5:16)

-A simple question from someone who got healed, lead to a whole day with miracles.

Set free
One day I was going to preach in a church in Norway.
I saw her right away when I entered the pulpit - the lady sitting in the back, just staring at the floor.
-Satan had bounded her.

It was only one thing to do. I walked over to her and asked if I could pray for her.
The smile she gave me, just told me that prayer was necessary.

I commanded Satan to leave her in Jesus' name.
After that, I comforted her with some words from the Bible.

One week later, I got a phone call from the same lady and told me the good news.

How she got my number, I do not know.

-When I heard her voice, I recognized it right away.

Her soft voice started to speak at the other end.

"Hello, it is me who you prayed for last week."

-Hello, I said, how are you?

Something good happened. 2-3 days after you prayed for me, different things started to happen.

I have struggled with depression for a long time. It has been horrible, but after you prayed for me, I have not been depressed, and I have been sleeping like a princess ever since.

-She said thank you over and over again.

Thank you, Lord.

The Shoemaker

They are unavoidable, the shoemakers that sit around the city square.

To preach the Gospel to the people working is not easy. Most of the time, they are busy.

Many times I have been bold and sneaked in a word or two about Jesus during their work, but almost every time I heard: "I am busy."

This day, I was carrying a big banner, and it was unavoidable for people to see it.

I walked up to the shoemakers and asked them once again a question.

-This time one of them said right away: "pain, pain and pointed to his back."

I lean over him and start praying.

-Suddenly he rose and began to dance like they did in the sixties and shouted: "it's gone, it's gone!" And he smiled like he had won the jackpot in the state lottery.

-Healed.

Jane

For a whole week, she had been struggling with back pain. The kind that makes you 90% handicapped. To put on shoes and go to the comfort room is suddenly of great difficulty. Not even her head, she was able to move around.

-There was no doubt that her pain was immense.

This day, my wife and I had been invited for lunch at her place. When we arrived, I took her aside and said I would pray for her. She told me that for four days, she had wanted to call me since she already knows that I am someone who prays for the sick.

"Why did you not call me?" I asked her.

"I don't know," she answered.

-Okay, I said, let me pray for you now.

In Jesus' name, I commanded the pain to leave her.

-Suddenly it was all silent. Then she started a back exercise that I've never seen before.

Are you okay now? I asked her.

-I think not yet, she replied.

I laid my hand on her back again, and gave thanks to the Lord, that by His stripes she had been healed. (1 Peter 2:24)

-Healed!

What a mighty God we have.

CHAPTER 10

Jesus

Jesus Christ; From the oldest, of the oldest of times.

He was foreknown before the foundation of the world was laid.
And for their sake, He has become apparent in the end.

"Who through Him believe in God, who raised Him from the
dead and gave Him glory so that your faith and hope are in
God." (1 Peter 1:21)

We are redeemed by the precious blood of Christ
"Knowing that you were not redeemed with corruptible things,
like silver or gold, from your aimless conduct received by tradition from your fathers, but with the precious blood of Christ, as
of a lamb without blemish and without spot." (1 Peter 1:18-19)

Jesus came for the sick, not the healthy ones
Today's supercilious (arrogant) Christians are not very interested
in continuing what Jesus Christ started with. Preaching the
Gospel and reaching out their hands to the lost ones.

The Pharisees and the scribes said to the disciples
Look, He eats and drinks with the tax collectors and the sinners.

"When Jesus heard it, He said to them,
those who are well have no need of a physician, but those who
are sick. I did not come to call the righteous, but sinners, to repentance." (Mark 2:17)

Jesus came for all the sinners to repentance
-What then is your task?
"Go into all the world and preach the gospel to every creature."
(Mark 16:15)

Jesus wants the sick to recover
-What then is your task?
"Lay your hands on the sick, and they will recover."
(Mark 16:18)

If Jesus was out there among the sinners, why are you not doing
the same?
Are you a Pharisee?

**It will not be easy to be a lukewarm Christian on the judg-
ment day.**

"But why do you call Me Lord, Lord, and not do the things
which I say?" (Luke 6:46)

"But He will say, I tell you I do not know you, where you are
from. Depart from Me, all you workers of iniquity."
(Luke 13:27)

The crucifixion of Jesus Christ was the universe biggest rescue mission

A rescue mission for all humanity.

We must take it

Repentance from all sins and turn to Christ Jesus as our Savior.

You and I, we have all sinned. This qualifies only to one thing, forever damnation in the lake of fire.

But the Lord wants everybody to come to the knowledge of the truth and to be saved.

"God our Savior, who desires all men to be saved and to come to the knowledge of the truth." (1 Timothy 2:3-4)

We (all Christians) are a part of the rescue mission that Christ did on Calvary.

-The Lord has commanded; Go into the entire world and preach the message of repentance and bring souls to heaven.

Nothing is more important than this.

The Bible says

-Not your kingdom, but the Lord's.

Only the Lord's Kingdom we shall build. Not our kingdoms as many 'churches' do today.

We choose selective who and where people shall sit in the boat, (church) and how they shall behave, who shall preach, and control upfront what people shall testify.

This we find absolutely no coverage for in God's written word.

We must step forward into the power of the Holy Ghost, and with the gifts of the Spirit, standing victoriously after overcoming everything in our Lord Jesus Christ's name. (Ephesians 6:13)

It is Christ Jesus, who is the door opener to Almighty God.

"Who through Him believe in God, who raised Him from the dead and gave Him glory, so that your faith and hope are in God." (1 Peter 1:21)

"Heaven and earth will pass away, but My words will by no means pass away." (Matthew 24:35)

We do not have access to Almighty God without Jesus Christ. (Ephesians 2:18)

You know Jesus because He chose to reveal Himself to you.

"All things have been delivered to Me by My Father, and no one knows who the Son is except the Father, and who the Father is except the Son, and the one to whom the Son wills to reveal Him." (Luke 10:22)

The mind of Christ
When injustice flows over the saints who are in the Lord's service, the Bible shows us how we should relate to it.

What God delights in, not this world's delights
"And do not be conformed to this world, but be transformed by the renewing of your mind, that you may prove what is that good and acceptable and perfect will of God." (Romans 12:2)

If they want to take what you have, let them take it
"If anyone wants to sue you and take away your tunic, let him have your cloak also." (Matthew 5:40)

Bless those who curse and destroy
"But I say to you, love your enemies, bless those who curse you, do good to those who hate you, and pray for those who spitefully use you and persecute you." (Matthew 5:44)

"Let this mind be in you which was also in Christ Jesus." (Philippians 2:5)

"For who has known the mind of the Lord that he may instruct Him? But we have the mind of Christ." (1 Corinthians 2:16)

"Therefore, if anyone is in Christ, he is a new creation; old things have passed away; behold, all things have become new." (2 Corinthians 5:17)

"Be of the same mind toward one another. Do not set your mind on high things, but associate with the humble. Do not be wise in your own opinion." (Romans 12:16)

Involve yourself
Nothing whatsoever will happen if you don't involve yourself.

-We must: involve ourselves in what the Bible says about sin.
-We must: involve ourselves in what the Bible says about repentance.
-We must: involve ourselves to build a personal relationship with Jesus.
-We must: implicate ourselves in God's written word.

A child can receive simple things, can you?

Hence, the scripture says
"God resists the proud, but give grace to the humble."
(James 4:6)

Lay down your life, pick up your cross daily
"Then Jesus said to His **disciples**, If anyone desires to come after Me, let him deny himself, and take up his cross, and follow Me." (Matthew 16:24)

The word **disciples** are from the Greek word **mathetes**. It means; Pupil, learner, disciple.

Believe God's written word and obey His commandments
This is what it takes to get a spiritual life.

Jesus Christ is the truth himself
"But the Helper, the Holy Spirit, whom the Father will send in My name, he will teach you all things, and bring to your remembrance all things that I said to you." (John 14:26)

Jesus says to the church today; Absolutely no compromise on My Gospel!

The 'church' answers;
No, we shall not speak in tongues: we might offend someone.
No, it is not proper to cast out demons when unsaved are around us.
No, we shall not 'all' go out into the streets and preach the Gospel. That is the work of an evangelist.

Today's church is full of the words No
Instead of being filled with a Holy Ghost Yes.

-Yes, to heal the sick.
-Yes to cast out demons wherever you are.
-Yes to speak in tongues, interpret and demonstrate God's Kingdom in front of others.
-Yes to preach with Holy Ghost power, so sinners understand they need a Savior! (Acts 2:29-39 - Pay attention to the first line in verse 37. "Cut to the heart." NKJV)

Think about it one more time
You have the same Spirit inside you that raised Jesus from the dead.

Jesus says; Go into all the world. But the Christians says; No I won't
Then it is straightforward to explain why there are so many immature Christians. You can never make a disciple if you are not willing to be one yourself.

This world is filled with sick people
Go and lay your hands on them; Go and preach the Gospel and
set the captives free.

We have all kinds of excuses and solutions for not going.
It doesn't require a lot of Biblical understanding to see that there
is something wrong with this picture.

**The fundamental truth of the Gospel; God makes unright-
eous people righteous.**

What does it mean to have Jesus Christ as Lord?
The word Lord means He who decides, He who determines.
If Jesus is your Lord, it is He who decides what you shall do. It
is He who is your boss.

How can Jesus be your Lord if you are not willing to do what
He says?
-Your flesh is your Lord.

Jesus intercedes for His children
He said; It is fulfilled and yielded up His Spirit.

But it did not end there
In the heavenly, Jesus continues His work for humanity.

Listen
"Therefore He is also able to save to the uttermost those who
come to God through Him, since He always lives to make inter-
cession for them." (Hebrews 7:25)

The invitation
Jesus Christ has given an invitation to all mankind; "Come to Me, all you who labor and are heavy laden, and I will give you rest." (Matthew 11:28)

No matter how many burdens or what sizes they are, or any kind of problems you have, God has an answer for you.
There is only one place where you can find solutions for your problems, and that is at the feet of Jesus Christ.

Out of your heart
"He who believes in Me, as the Scripture has said, out of his heart will flow rivers of living water." (John 7:38)

The Father gave it all to His Son
"And Jesus came and spoke to them, saying, all authority has been given to Me in heaven and earth." (Matthew 28:18)

God is watching everything everywhere
"The eyes of the Lord are in every place, keeping watch on the evil and the good." (Proverbs 15:3)

If anyone thirst
"On the last day, that great day of the feast, Jesus stood and cried out, saying, If anyone thirsts, let him come to Me and drink." (John 7:37)

Influenced by traditions, as well as an unbelieving attitude toward God, man has changed God to; He was.

Always give thanks to the Father

"And whatever you do in the word of the deed, do all in the name of the Lord Jesus, giving thanks to God the Father through Him." (Colossians 3:17)

The wisdom has been with God from eternity

"The Lord possessed me at the beginning of His way, before His works of old. I have been established from everlasting, from the beginning, before there was ever an earth. When there were no depths I was brought forth, when there were no fountains abounding with water. Before the mountains were settled, before the hills, I was brought forth; while as yet He had not made the earth or the fields, or the primal dust of the world. When He prepared the heavens, I was there, when he drew a circle on the face of the deep, when He established the clouds above, when He strengthened the fountains of the deep, when He assigned to the sea its limit, so that the waters would not transgress His command, when He marked out the foundations of the earth, then I was beside Him as a master craftsman, and I was daily His delight, rejoicing always before Him." (Proverbs 8:22-30)

Jesus is the wisdom, and happy is he who finds it

"Blessed is the man who listens to me, watching daily at my gates, waiting at the posts of my doors, for whoever finds me finds life, and obtains favor from the Lord." (Proverbs 8:34-35)

The written word of God is His voice

"In the beginning was the Word, and the Word was with God, and the Word was God." (John 1:1)

With raised hands

When you praise the Lord when you sing to Him.

It is not only with a raised hand and a resounding amen we shall praise the Lord.
-Let us have a closer look at what is written in James 1:27, King James version.

"Pure religion and undefiled before God and the Father is this, To visit the fatherless and widows in their affliction, and to keep himself unspotted from the world." (James 1:27)

The second word in this verse is **religion**. What does this word mean? Religion from Greek means; Ceremonial observance - worshipping.

The next word, **fatherless**, is from the Greek word **orphanos**, and it means; Parentless, uncomfort, fatherless.
We also find the word **widow**. Widow is from the Greek word **chera**, and it means; A widow. (As lacking a husband)

This is basically what James 1:27 teaches us; **Visit the father-less and widows in their distress**.
-Now you have the revelation about it. Be bold enough to act on it.

"Love your neighbor as yourself." (Matthew 22:39)

"Do not be afraid; I am the first and the Last. I am He who lives, and was dead, and behold, I am alive forevermore. Amen. And I have the keys of Hades and of Death." (Revelation 1:17-18)

The Bible says

He is the king of justice. He is King of times. He is the king of heaven. He is the king of kings and the Lord of Lord's. He is impartially merciful. He is the Son of God. He is the sinner's Savior.

He is the centerpiece of civilization.
He is the fundamental doctrine of true theology. He guards, and He guides. He heals the sick. He cleans leprosy. He forgives sinners. He defends the week. He rewards the diligent. He is the key to knowledge. He is the source of wisdom. He is the way to peace. His goodness is boundless. His mercy endures forever. His love never changes. His grace is sufficient. His yoke is easy. His burdens are light. He is irresistible!
You cannot get Him out of your mind. You cannot live without Him.

The Pharisees hated Him.
But they found out that they could not stop Him.

Pilate found no fault with Him. Herod could not kill Him. Death could not handle Him. The grave could not hold Him.

Our Lord and Savior, Jesus Christ, who gave His life that we might have life.

CHAPTER 11

Brothers and Sisters

The product of disobedience

They have gone to 'churches' for years. Many of them do not apprehend why they have never experienced the power of the Holy Ghost, miracles, and healings. They see someone on a pulpit, and they feel the presence of the Lord, but somehow they think all of this is from the Lord.

An 'anointed' preacher comes to your church - fellowship. He lay his hands on your head, so you fall right away under the 'anointing.'

Is this important? Is this what we want when it comes to Christianity?
Do we want a touch and fall ministry?

Today's prominent Christians travel from one place that is filled with believers to another.
-Christians preach to Christians all the time.

Is this our primary work for the Lord?

Or have we forgotten that Jesus Christ's Atonement at the Cross of the Calvary, was a reconciliation work between God and man?

-The sinful man that Jesus of all His heart wants to be saved.

Are we going to take the Lord seriously?

Or shall we run to church every Sunday to have 'touch' from a preacher who says: This is God touching you.

The Holy Ghost, as described in the Bible, is the One who shall help you to get the work done.

The work that is described in Matthew 28:19-20 - Mark 16:15. To preach the Gospel to a **lost world**.

Let the Lord be the center in the Sunday meetings; Be a disciple that follows the Lord - not the adventures itself.

A fellowship of carnal desires

Some call it a cell group, Lifeline, or Bible study.

Whatever work you have in this world today, effectivity is of paramount importance. There is absolutely no limit to how effective we have to be in our work. 'Time is money,' they say.

Committees have been made to make the most effective time schedules. This may be ok if you own an airline company or two.

If you use the method of time scheduling like what this world does and bring it into your fellowship, it will be nothing else than a worldly meeting filled the work of the flesh.

The Holy Ghost does not let anyone control him with time schedules.

-Those who arrange this kind of meetings are not spiritually mature.

The Holy Ghost is unwanted

They think they have a church. But are they seeking the Lord about what church is? Is church something we shall have, or shall we be the church? No matter congregation or building, it is never a church if it does not follow the Lord's commandments in the Bible.

If you are someone who represents the Lord, you must come as a humble representative of the Lord. Not someone who has your bag filled with printed sermons from the Internet, and a jam-packed schedule.

It is terrible when Christians try to spiritualize the works of the flesh.

Where 2 or 3 are gathered, the Lord is in the middle, they say

And the Bible says that. But is it enough that the Lord is there? Cause if He is there as number one for the whole congregation, the power of the Holy Ghost is there. And if the power is there, God will move in the directions that He wants. But time schedules and printed teachings from the Internet hinders the Lord to move.

Jesus wants to be number one in all people's life. If we do not let Him be number one, He will never be number one.
-God does not force anyone.

The evangelist, today's 'church' do not want them
God has given the church the evangelist as a teacher. To teach the church about the deeps of Jesus Christ, and to equip the people to function in healing, miracles, and preaching the Gospel with Holy Ghost power.

To walk in the Spirit is to go out
If you are not carrying fruit to others, you are not walking in the Spirit.

"For out of the abundance of the heart his mouth speaks."
(Luke 6:45)

If you act on what the scriptures say, the Scripture will become alive.

It was out there Jesus said;
"Those who are well have no need of a physician, but those who are sick." (Matthew 9:12)

If the Lord says that all who do not know Him is sick, what are we doing when we stand in church on Sundays, with lifted hands, and ask the Lord to send the unsaved into the church?

The unsaved do not come to today's churches.

The Lord said; Go out into the whole world and preach the Gospel.
-The 'church' says; No - You must send them here.
-Something is terribly wrong with this picture.

Luke 15
Let us have a look at what is written in verse one; "Then all the tax collectors and the sinners drew near to Him to hear Him."

All the sinners came
Why did they come? Cause the light and the power was there. Are you the light as the Bible says you shall be? If not, get out there and be the light for those who live in darkness.

If you believe and act on the word of God, then the Holy Ghost power will be there
The believers that the Lord is with, there it is power, revelations from Scripture, healings, deliverances, miracles.

If we are in a church that builds its kingdom, there is little power or no power at all.
Fleshly manifestations are all there is.

On the tree, you shall know its fruits. What fruits? That's the fruits of the Holy Ghost. And He only follows the written word of Almighty God. (Luke 12:33)

Jesus went to the dead.
To Lazarus, He went. Imagine all the infidels the Lord had around Him on this day.

Jesus was with the prostitutes and tax collectors. Imagine the religious Pharisees said when they mocked Jesus; why is your master is eating with tax collectors and sinners. (Matthew 9:11)

Today's pharisaic churches

Let us have a look at this example; Have you tried to say to your congregation/fellowship that you will cancel your holiday to Hawaii, the all-inclusive four-star Hotel, that was recommended to you from one of the church leaders. Because you have decided to go to Pattaya Thailand instead?

That you have ordered a room in a one-star hotel in the middle of the red light district downtown Pattaya, with nothing included except a full view of at least 10 bars with high healed workers, that works 24/7, all year.

But think what the leaders in your church will say?

Instead, think what Jesus has said; "Those who are well have no need of a physician, but those who are sick." (Matthew 9:12)

If you say this to the controlling religious believers in your fellowship, they will fall off the chair before you are finished talking.

Let us look at a couple of things that are quite interesting

If there is anyone who needs a physician in Pattaya, it is the girls that work on the bars. Most of them are willing to do almost everything for nearly nothing.

Those who work on the streets are most of the time, the ones who cannot work in a bar because the bars demand health certificates. Then it is a big chance that most of them that are on the streets are sick.

In the middle of this, we, as born-again Christian, really have a chance to show them who the Lord is. Think of what it is written in the last line in Exodus 15:26. "For I am the Lord who **heals** you."
Heals, from the Hebrew word; **Rapha'**.

And here is a revelation of the word **Rapha'**; **The Lord that manifests Himself through healing**.
-Think about it, what an enormous promise.

Imagine yourself downtown Pattaya, and you lay your hands on an H.I.V positive. This person is healed from this terrible sickness. You preach with Holy Ghost power, and the person receives.

Now you are a part of the gigantic rescue mission that Jesus Christ did for humanity on Calvary.

Imagine this
Under a bridge in Pattaya, a lady is standing. Maybe she has been raped several times in the last months. Perhaps she has a little child at home who screams of starvation. The husband or boyfriend left them a long time ago, and her old mother on 80 is the daily/nightly babysitter. There are absolutely no social systems that they can rely on.

Is she a sinner? Yes, but did not Jesus said that He came for the one who is living in darkness? Did He not tell all the Christians to go out into the entire world, preach the Gospel, heal the sick, and set the captives free?

Are not we all a part of; **Go into all the world?**
-Are not all the people that are working on the 'streets' a part of all the world?

If your wife - husband does not allow you to go and preach to the girls in Pattaya, there are plenty of men in the same 'business.'

Imagine what a powerful tool you have when you reach out to this lady that is raped and abused.

Imagine what a great God we have that says: I have not come for the healthy but the sick.

If this is something for you, get online and order tickets.

It will be an uproar in your fellowship
But the sounds of the feet that walk with the Lord's Gospel is more beautiful than the most exceptional symphony concert.

The Pharisees in your fellowship will shout to you
The ones who are captured in prostitution will also shout; Except they will scream; HELP.

When you are in the downtown of Pattaya, it is not only the ladies with high heels you will meet. In Thailand, like many other places in Asia, a lot of disabled people are abandoned. You will find them in the streets next to the ladies with high heels. **-They are left to themselves**.

There are no social systems that would take care of them. Most of the time, they are staying where the tourists are, playing an instrument for you to donate a coin or two, for them to survive.

For us who are born again, it does not matter if we have sex temptations around us when we live a life close to the Lord. But, if you have not laid down your life entirely to Him, a senior center in your neighborhood is a more suitable place to preach.

Everything is a terrible battle, just to survive
They do not see the light, only the darkness. But you shall come as the light! (Matthew 5:13-14)

In the darkness, you shall be the light
"Let your light so shine before men, that they may see your good works and glorify your Father in heaven." (Matthew 5:16)

The Gospel you represent, the power you demonstrate. Praised be our Lord and Savior Jesus Christ.

Where you are trained
It is crucial how you are trained by the Holy Ghost, to be a Christian that bears fruit. It is vital that we use Jesus as an example of how He did this, not what the pastor or the leaders in

your fellowship means. You must start to work where there is a need. Places where people need the true Jesus Christ.

It is not only the Jesus that loves us but the One who gave His life for humanity.
-He is the Deliverer. He is the healer. He is the Savior. He is the God of love and wrath. He is the one who is willing to forgive those who are willing to repent from their sinful lives.

To achieve this, you must be born again. You must be free from this world and the church's yoke.
You must not accept anything that is thrown unto you from any brother or sister.

When you start to pray for the sick and miracles start to happen, you will encounter something strange.
In your fellowship, you might be unpopular, but the unsaved will love you.
-That I can tell you from my own experiences.

Jesus Christ, this world's spokesman in front of the Father
"My little children, these things I write to you, so that you may not sin. And if anyone sins, we have an Advocate with the Father, Jesus Christ the righteous. And He is the propitiation for our sins, and not for ours only but also the whole world."
(1 John 2:1-2)

"For God so loved the world that He gave His only begotten Son, that whoever believes in Him should not perish but have everlasting life." (John 3:16)

CHAPTER 12

Kingdoms

Human being

A master builder without equal. We build and build, we travel to the moon, and soon maybe the travel companies have star tours to Mars.

Nonetheless, what kind of kingdom is humanity trying to build? Is it the Lord's kingdom? No.

Our own kingdom that is what we have become specialists in building.

You may like it or not, but this world's party and tragedies will soon be over

The time that we are living in now is heading towards judgment day.

Let all the positive prophets talk about upswings, let all the pastors and politicians proclaim their optimistic messages.

The end

This world lives in a feast and debauchery. Soon you shall leave the party and stand in front of the Lord your God and be held accountable for everything you have said and done.

(Hebrews 9:27 - Revelation 20:12)

There is a drought in several places in the world. It is economic chaos in other areas. Greedy culture spreads all over, and it is me, myself, and I that counts.

"That this is a rebellious people, lying children, children who not hear the law of the Lord." (Isaiah 30:9)

When a society becomes rich and prosperous, it becomes blind regarding their spiritual situation.
-We are rich and lacks nothing.

But the Bible says
"Riches do not profit in the day of wrath, but righteousness delivers from death." (Proverbs 11:4)

Fear God, and He will train you up
"The fear of the Lord is the beginning of wisdom: A good understanding have all those who do His commandments. His praise endures forever." (Psalm 111:10)

We have all wandered away from the Lord
"All we like sheep have gone astray; we have turned, everyone, to his own way; And the Lord has laid on Him the iniquity of us all." (Isaiah 53:6)

Life must be laid down for the Lord
Your life in this world must be lived as one who is born again. You cannot continue to live in with the works of the flesh. But a new life, as one who is born again from heaven.

When you are born again, you shall no longer take after this world. But follow the Lord and His commandments.

"Beware lest anyone cheat you through philosophy and empty deceit, according to the tradition of men, according to the basic principles of the world, and not according to Christ."
(Colossians 2:8)

Imagine the following
If everyone who was born again took the Lord's commandments seriously, the world would not be as it is today.
The probability that Jesus had already returned would have been great.

But most of the believers are having more than enough with its own life, and the Lord's day (which is every day) is graded down to a miserable Sunday. Yes, they pray and speak to the Lord, but then again, obeying the mission commandment, living in holiness, raising others to victory are not many who have faith for or willingness to do.
-If they do not have faith in this, what do they have faith for then?

Their kingdom, not the Lord's
If the Lord says; You must be born again to see the kingdom of God, (John 3:3), then we must grasp it and be born again. But most of us continued to live in this world, and not according to the Lord.

"Most assuredly, I say to you, unless one is born again, he cannot see the kingdom of God." (John 3:3)

In John 3:3, we read the word **see**.
See is from the Greek word **eido**, and it means; To know, be aware, can tell, be sure, have the knowledge, understand.

We read further in Romans 10:13, "For whoever calls on the name of the Lord shall be **saved**."

The word saved is from the Greek word **Sozo**. It means; To save, rescued, heal, preserve, be (make) whole.

If you shall be someone who establishes God's kingdom here on earth, why would you continue to live after this worlds' principles?
-It is here that everything slips. The Lord is a Lord of miracles: it is not just healing we are talking about.

Look at Moses at the red sea. They had a problem. This world was after them and wanted to kill all of them. But the Lord had another plan, and that plan depended on Moses' obedience.

Moses believed and acted on the mandate that the Lord had given him. I am not sure if he knew what he did, but he obeyed, and the sea was divided.
Then the Lord could act through Moses' faith. The Lord of miracles divided the sea, and everyone could walk over.

Today

What about us believers today? Do we believe that the Lord is the God of miracles?

Do we believe that He is capable of solving every problem in this world today? Do you think that your problems are too big for the Lord to solve? The biggest problem is if you are willing to humble yourself in front of the Lord.

-Your humbleness and faith in front of the Lord. Your daily breakdown of the flesh, which all believers must live in.

Do not love the world

"Do not love the world or the things in the world. If anyone loves the world, the love of the Father is not in him. For all that is in the world, the lust of the flesh, the lust of the eyes, and the pride of life is not of the Father but is of the world. And the world is passing away, and the lust of it; but he who does the will of God abides forever." (1 John 2:15-17)

For all that is in the world

Think about it. All.

Most of us have heard sermons on carnal desires.

But look at what is written in the same verse: lust of the eyes. Everything that we are exposed to every day.

Just look at the tv channels. Every 10 minutes, it is a dozen commercials. And it runs 24/7.

Our mailboxes are filled daily with; 'you must buy this' advertisements.

You are exposed to the actions of the unbelievers every day.
Everything from short skirts to the latest and best bottle of co-
gnac, with 'only' 40% alcohol content.

It is written in Joshua 1:8
"This Book of the Law shall not depart from your mouth, but
you shall meditate in it day and night, that you may observe to
do according to all that is written in it. For then you will make
your way prosperous, and then you will have good success."

What a wonderful promise. Here says the Lord, if you are willing to obey His written word, then you will make your way
prosperous, and then you will have good success.
-Then, strangely, we do not choose that direction with all our
heart, mind, and soul.

"You shall love the Lord your God with all your heart, with all
your soul, and with all your mind." (Matthew 22:37)

Carrier chased
Before the roster is up, we are up jogging and everything else
than the Lord's will. We filled our brains with so much 'knowledge' that we do not enter the presence of the Lord, or hear His
voice.

One day I was watching a video on YouTube. It was a young
man from the U.S.A. who had found economic success. And
now he was eager to tell everybody about his formula. He had
lived in the countryside, and almost given up for his 47 dollars
in his pocket. One day he had hitchhiked to a big city and started

to fill himself with knowledge from books. Many kinds of books, the Bible was never mentioned.

He recorded this video in his garage in Beverly Hills next to his Lamborghini and 2000 books.

-Boldly, he shared about his success.

He had read one book every single day since the day that he had left his hometown a long time ago. The knowledge from the books had led him out of poverty and into financial wealth.

But what does God Yahweh say about this?
-Knowledge shall be great in the last days.

"But you, Daniel, shut up the words, and seal the book until the time of the end; many shall run to and fro, and knowledge shall increase." (Daniel 12:4)

"And because lawlessness will abound, the love of many will grow cold." (Matthew 24:12)

The fear of the Lord is the beginning of knowledge.
(Proverbs 1:7)

The knowledge that is in this world will not help you much in the work of the Lord.

Jesus told the rich man to sell everything and give it to the poor.
In return, he would be given a treasure in heaven.
But he went away sorrowful, for he had great possessions.

"And again I say to you, it is easier for a camel to go through the eye of a needle than for a rich man to enter the kingdom of God." (Matthew 19:24)

God says one thing, humanity says something else
Pride and control is not a surrendered life to the Lord.
Most people do not want anything to do with the Lord, and they want to walk their ways. No savior they need because they already have what they 'think' they need.
-Freedom to do whatever they want.

God warns us about pitfalls; A man says that he has enough knowledge to put a lid over all pitfalls.

Extreme materialism exists in parts of the world today
"But know this, that in the last days perilous times will come: For men will be lovers of themselves, lovers of money, boasters, proud, blasphemers, disobedient to parents, unthankful, unholy, unloving, unforgiving, slanderers, without self-control, brutal, despisers of good, traitors, headstrong, haughty, lovers of pleasure rather than lovers of God, having a form of godliness but denying its power. **And from such people turn away!**"
(2 Timothy 3:1-5)

It is the end of heavenly knowledge if we do not fear the Lord
Then the demons of knowledge will take over. And they have only one thing to present; to steal, to kill, and to destroy everything.

We believe the only solution is the one we have, and religion is something terrible because we have seen that in the news.
-This world's news should be called: 'This world's unnecessary tragedies.'

It is Jesus we need
"I am the way, the truth, and the life. No one comes to the Father except through Me." (John 14:6)

God is a jealous God
It is you He wants, the whole you, all the time, Jesus Christ wants to fellowship with you and me. (Exodus 20:5)

A religious man says: You shall not, you cannot, not like that, we must be careful, so we do not..!
This is not of the Holy Ghost but a religious spirit.

The Holy Ghost shall teach us all things
A good teacher never uses a hammer. But he begins by explaining how it is and how it shall be done.

-He will show through scripture. (Revelations)
When it is like this, it is of the Holy Ghost and not of a religious spirit that has no other plan than to tie you up, so you are unable to receive any revelation from the Lord.

Stop looking at the preacher, keep your eyes on the Lord
For years, Christians have attended meetings and conventions. They travel to hear one 'anointed' preacher after the other. But what will they accomplish with this?

-Is it the Lord they need, or is it something missing in their own lives?

There is nothing wrong with attending meetings or conventions.
-But why?
Is it to get hold of the latest teaching, or is it because the Bible says we shall not stop meeting each other?
I think all of us daily must take a closer look at what we see in the mirror.

Money or the truth?
What do people want? Do they want an ocean of money, or do they want the truth?

Most people think that the truth lies in money. They believe this is where deliverance is, and this is where life begins to make sense. If they have enough money, they are free to do whatever they want.

Throughout the years, I have met many Christians who are bound by the economy. Many of them state: If I only have that much, then I should have done this and that.

Circumstances do not bring freedom in Christ; Only the obedience to the word of the Lord.

The Bible says
"No one can serve two masters; for either he will hate the one and love the other, or else he will be loyal to the one and despise

the other. You cannot serve God and **mammon**."
(Matthew 6:24)

Mammon means confidence in wealth, money.

Most of us are involved in the race after more money
We all need money, but how much do we need? And how much
of our free time, shall we waste chasing more paper?

There is a heaven waiting for us.
There is a God who is longing more than we can imagine having
a fellowship with us.
-Take it now. Don't wait any longer!

**"And you shall know the truth, and the truth shall make you
free."** (John 8:32)

Notes;

_____

_____

_____

_____

_____

_____

140

Notes;

_____

_____

_____

_____

_____

_____

_____

_____

_____

_____

_____

_____

CHAPTER 13

This world's content

Humanity's justified decisions and proclamations
People have habits. And our habits are of many different things.
What we think are; **Creatures of habit**.
And we speak out that we are a creature of habits. This we proclaim to justify our busy life.

This justification of ourselves is a result of our failure in discerning the thoughts that come to us.
It is in our thoughts where Satan has his workplace. If we do not have any spiritual understanding of what is going on here, all of us became victims of Satan's deceitful plans.

Satan sends his seductive thoughts, and we grasp them quickly because we think that we are a habit creature.
The Bible does not say we are a 'habit' creature, but that we are created in God's image.

In His image
"So God created man in His own image; in the image of God He created him; male and female He created them." (Genesis 1:27)

That's what people are, neither more nor less.

We tend to cling towards our habits. We go to the same stores, and we drive the same way every time.

What does the Bible tell us about the openness and boldness the Lord gave us?

If the Lord gave us free will, why do we all run on the same tracks every day?

Statements such as

We are creatures of habit, is nothing else a justification of our fleshly desires in our lives.

The Bible says that if we believe the Lord and His written word, this is what walking on water is.

-Trust the Lord and His promises. His promises not to worry about tomorrow.

"Therefore do not worry about tomorrow, for tomorrow will worry about its own things. Sufficient for the day is its own trouble." (Matthew 6:34)

Man, trust entirely on their emotions

Many Christians trust entirely on their feelings. They claim that they are living with the Lord, and they go to 'church' every Sunday. When you speak with them, it is the victory, and they live in the presence of the Lord every day.

-But, suddenly, something happens.

Misunderstandings in the family, a new girlfriend before the old one has left the building, drinking on the weekends. Yes, the list is dark and long.

-Backbiting in the private life and congregation.
Proud as roosters while they are disobedient to God's Holy
Bible.
-It can be written books about human emotions and evil acts.

They are uninterested in the Lord's commandments. Themselves
in their world goes forward like a locomotive.

What is it the Lord means when He tells us not to trust our feelings?
What do people do when they choose to trust their feelings instead of the written word of Almighty God?

**Go into your prayer chamber, pray to the Lord, and get the
answers.**

The Bible says
"But you, when you pray, go into your room, and when you
have shut your door, pray to your Father who is in the secret
place; and your Father who sees in secret will reward you openly." (Matthew 6:6)

When we make a god in our head, we became religious like the
Pharisees.
Satan sends his evil thoughts, man thinks about it a second or
two, accept it, and then it gives birth to sin, then we fall. It is
terrible that we have not come further.

**Do not expect personal revival with this kind of perception
of everyday life.**

It is not strange at all when the Lord says: "I resist the proud."
(James 4:6)

This world solitude
The newspaper in Norway wrote this;

**-Norway has an invisible public health problem. Four out of
the ten youths and elders are now lonely.**

These are some of the points that the newspaper wrote about.

1. Loneliness is as harmful as smoking.

The Bible says:
"Come to Me, all you who labor and are heavy laden, and I will
give you rest." (Matthew 11:28)

2. You will be more vulnerable to getting diseases.

As believers, we will; Bind this false prophesy that is spoken
unto us in Jesus' Name. I do not accept it.

"Assuredly, I say to you, whatever you bind on earth will be
bound in heaven, and whatever you loose on earth will be loosed
in heaven." (Matthew 18:18)

In Jesus Name, we break every curse that is spoken to us.
We never accept this kind of statement that is directed against
us.

3. Social media can alleviate the problems.

The Bible says to have fellowship with each other.
"For where two or three are gathered together in My name, I am there in the midst of them." (Matthew 18:20)

It is always interesting to see who has been interviewed for a story like this. In this one, a homosexual male couple living together.

-A 'couple' that has chosen not at all to believe God. They deny the Lord, who has created them.
No matter what comes out of these people's mouth, is not the will of the Lord.

"Do you not know that the unrighteous will not inherit the kingdom of God? Do not be deceived. Neither fornicators, nor idolaters, nor adulterers, nor homosexuals, nor sodomites, nor thieves, nor covetous, nor drunkards, nor revilers, nor extortioners will inherit the kingdom of God." (1 Corinthians 6:9-10)

What is the final answer to these statements? People are enormously far away from God.

Jesus Christ is the ultimate and only answer to what people need in this world. The world that just gets darker and darker. He is the real God who gave His life on the Cross for the sins of this world: He who nailed His only Begotten Son for us to have an opportunity to repent of our sins and turn to Jesus Christ for our salvation.

It is the prince of this world (Satan) people have as Lord. He who is only here to steal, kill and destroy. (John 10:10)

Jesus says; Come to me
All who carry heavy laden, (Matthew 11:28) because I am the way the truth and the life. No one comes to the Father except through me. (John 14:6)

"I have come that they may have life and that they may have it more abundantly." (John 10:10)

The Gospel offers the power to live a clean life
"Therefore, having these promises, beloved, let us cleanse ourselves from all filthiness of the flesh and spirit, perfecting holiness in the fear of God." (2 Corinthians 7:1)

This world's loneliness is not the will of the Lord
God, our Savior, who desires all men to be saved and to come to the knowledge of the truth. (1 Timothy 2:3-4)

Man must repent, grab Jesus, and became born again.

"Most assuredly, I say to you, unless one is born again, he cannot see the kingdom of God." (John 3:3)

This is the only way to get a living relationship with Jesus Christ, our Messiah.

Do not search in this world

All the time, we are reminded of all the material things that we 'need' and 'must' have.

We 'must' perform in all things that we are involved in. Otherwise, we are not a part of 'that' world.

Everyone in this world that is not born again does not understand that Christians shall not follow this waltz that Satan is the producer of.

Only you can decide if you shall follow the Lord's ways or the ways of this world.

Wicked people distort God's grace

"For certain men have crept in unnoticed, who long ago were marked out for this condemnation, ungodly men, who turn the grace of our God into lewdness and deny the only Lord God and our Lord Jesus Christ." (Jude 4)

Depraved people

"Having a form of godliness but denying its power. And from such people turn away!" (2 Timothy 3:5)

"They profess to know God,

but in works they deny Him, being abominable, disobedient, and disqualified for every good work." (Titus 1:16)

"And because lawlessness will abound, the love of many will grow cold." (Matthew 24:12)

"Let no one deceive you with empty words, for because of these things the wrath of God comes upon the sons of disobedience. Therefore do not be partakers with them." (Ephesians 5:6-7)

Lust of the flesh = our carnal desires
"For all that is in the world, the lust of the flesh, the lust of the eyes, and the pride of life is not of the Father but is of the world." (1 John 2:16)

Spiritual replenishments
Christians travel to meetings and conventions. Many of those are coming to get 'refills.'
They live far into the carnal world; They fill themselves so much with this world that they 'need' spiritual replenishment. But this is not what they primarily seek. They seek something that can satisfy their conscience.
Just to be able to continue to fill themselves up with these things from this world.

Example
A guy was reading his Bible for an hour or two. An incredible presence of the Lord was there at that moment. But after his Bible study, the same person starts to fill himself with things of this world. TV series or other kinds of time thieves.
The Lord shows up in the Bible study, and we respond with pushing Him out again?
This is a picture that any lust of the flesh must be fought.

If we go to prayer meetings or big campaigns, we should arrive there overflowing.

Overflowed with the Holy Ghost to give unto others.

Very little are we able to handle a Holy presence of God. So much do we control our carnal desires!

We allow ourselves to be controlled. We allow Satan to have a strategic highway of thoughts that we just 'accept.'
This is a result of people who are not rooted in God's word. If you are not rooted in the word, then you do not know what to do when spiritual storms come. You think you know, but the fruit of your spiritual life shows the opposite.

Is it strange there is no revival among believers? No.

The Bible says; Do not take after this world.
-This is precisely what we are not doing.
Christians are standing in meetings and shouts; It is victory.
Most of them do not know what they are talking about.
There is little doubt that these people are very bound by the flesh and the powers in their thoughts.

Cold shock
Many travels far to their work. In the U.S.A., which is a vast country in size, they are used to travel long distances to their work. Under most of the bridges they are passing to their work, thousands of people have their 'homes.'
Those who pass over, have no relation to what is 'under' these bridges. Most people have their opinion about what is going on under the bridges, and they think if you give these people food or clothes, they will be even lazier to find work.

Very few are interested in these lost sheep.

Sin by Silence
"Therefore, to him who knows to do good and does not do it, to him it is a sin." (James 4:17)

What happens when you start to reach out to the lost?
-Will you encounter drug addicts? Yes.
-Will you encounter prostitutes? Yes.
-Will you encounter thieves and bandits? Yes.
-Will you encounter people who have broken most of the laws? Yes.
That's great! It is precisely what we read about in the gospels. Jesus did it. Now it is your turn.

Out there are those who do evil and are spiritually blind. Go and do what Jesus did.

The power of God, where you are
"Then all the tax collectors and the sinners drew near to Him to hear Him." (Luke 15:1)

This scripture tells us that they drew near Him. They gathered where the light was. The love in this world has not only become cold. It has a cold shock.
And this happened because people choose to live a sinful life. They push the Lord out, and everything else in.

What about you? Are you out among the poor reaching out your hands?

In prison

We borrow money, all the way to the rooftop.

We feel we must have that nice car and a nice house. But inside of us, we want something, but it's not sure the materialistic things are the right solutions.

-We feel safe, and we feel we must do what everybody else does.

-We feel we must have fellowship with something. But not with our creator, who created everything.

When it comes to our daily work, of course, it has to be 5-6 days a week and overtime now and then.

Is it wrong to work? No. But what says the scripture about your everyday life?

Go into the entire world, preach the Gospel, and make disciples. On the way, you reach out to the poor and needy ones.

This does not happen since we choose to work the same way as this world does.

First I, only my, mine and some more, please.

Not only in prison but captured inside of a prison

You are caught in a way that you cannot even move inside your prison. Satan has tied you up so hard that you cannot see the joy of your 'things.' Every day, all day is a battle to survive the battle of the mortgages.

"The wicked in his proud countenance does not seek God. God is none of his thoughts." (Psalm 10:4)

152

Notes;

CHAPTER 14

The Devil

Memories

They are good to have. But when they come in a way that hinders your breakthrough with the Lord, they are no longer just memories. Satan uses your memory bank to hinder what you are standing in faith for and having a breakthrough in.

Let us take a look at this example;

The silence has descended over your house. You are ready to lay your head on the pillow. Maybe you are using the time from you go to bed until you fall asleep as a quiet time before the Lord. You lay down, and silence descended upon you. You are ready for more even if you lay down to sleep. The streams of thoughts are slowing down, and all you did was acting on Matthew 6:6 - go into your room and close the door.

-Then it happens; There comes a thought from the past, and a positive thought about someone whom you had a good relationship with.

When thoughts come like this, then it is from Satan. You may think now that this cannot be right because there is nothing wrong with thinking positive about someone, that you never had any misunderstanding with. But if you have decided to spend the time before your sleep in the presence of the Lord, then you shall be quiet in front of Him as it is written in Matthew 6:6.

Satan hates this

He hates the fact that you try to enter the presence of the Lord. What does he do then? He gives you positive thoughts from the past, and you accept them because you think they are 'good.' The result is that you missed the presence of the Lord because you choose the other thoughts.

You fall asleep, thinking that you have done the right thing. You got tempted, and you lost. Satan wins and is laughing with triumph.

If we do not grow in the understanding of what is written in 2 Corinthians 10:5, then we will never understand how Satan can destroy our walk with the Lord.

Listen;

"Casting down arguments and every high thing that exalts itself against the knowledge of God, bringing every thought into captivity to the obedience of Christ." (2 Corinthians 10:5)

In the times that we are living now, we must stop to seek the 'experiences' and enter into an understanding of how spiritual things are functioning.

Obedience to God's written word is the only thing which we shall relate to.

The author of misery, sorrows, sicknesses, and pain
"Whose minds the god of this age has blinded. Who do not believe, lest the light of the gospel of the glory of Christ, who is the image of God, should shine on them." (2 Corinthians 4:4)

Satan's only wish and plan is to destroy human lives to bring sorrow to God, our Fathers' heart.

"He who accused them before our God day and night!"
(Revelation 12:10)

"Be sober, be vigilant; because your adversary the devil walks about like a roaring lion, seeking whom he may devour."
(1 Peter 5:8)

Be vigilant. What does it mean?
Simply said from the Greek translation; Stay awake. Be in a (spiritual) position so you will be able to understand what is going on at all times.

Capture every thought (reveal Satan's cunning mind attacks) under the obedience of Christ.

The Tempter
"Now when the tempter came to Him, he said, if you are the Son of God, command that these stones become bread."
(Matthew 4:3)

An excellent example that the Pharisees did not recognize the Lord

"Now when the Pharisees heard it they said, This fellow does not cast out demons except by Beelzebub, the ruler of the demons." (Matthew 12:24)

"In which you once walked according to the course of this world, according to the prince of the power of the air, the spirit who now works in the sons of disobedience." (Ephesians 2:2)

"I will no longer talk much with you, for the ruler of this world is coming, and he has nothing in Me." (John 14:30)

"But I fear, lest somehow, as the serpent deceived Eve by his craftiness, so your minds may be corrupted from the simplicity that is in Christ." (2 Corinthians 11:3)

Here, we see that the thoughts become corrupted.
It is of great importance that I mention again, to get into a spiritual understanding as the scripture says.

"Having disarmed principalities and powers, He made a public spectacle of them, triumphing over them in it."
(Colossians 2:15)

Your fight with Satan will not be over before he is in the lake of fire

Jesus made a public spectacle of them. Now you must act on what Jesus has opened up for. He gave you the authority to trample on snakes and scorpions.

"Behold, I give you the authority to trample on serpents and scorpions, and over <u>all</u> the **power** of the enemy, and nothing shall by any means hurt you." (Luke 10:19)

The word **power** is from the Greek word **Dunamis**. It means; Worker of miracles, strength.

Satan will operate in miracles

If you discern, you will reveal what is of the Holy Ghost, and what is from Satan and the demons.
If we do not enter into the spiritual authority that is given to us, then we will fall.

"Nor give place to the devil." (Ephesians 4:27)

If you give Satan place in your thoughts, he will get a hold of you.
This you can not allow.

Eternal punishment and God's wrath

"He who believes in the Son has everlasting life, and he who does not believe the Son shall not see life, but the wrath of God abides on him." (John 3:36)

Eternal damnation

"These shall be punished with everlasting destruction from the presence of the Lord and from the glory of His power."
(2 Thessalonians 1:9)

Eternal death

"For the wages of sin is death, but the gift of God is eternal life in Christ Jesus our Lord." (Romans 6:23)

Hell

"If your right eye causes you to sin, pluck it out and cast it from you; for it is more profitable for you that one of your members perish, than for your whole body to be cast into hell."
(Matthew 5:29)

"Serpents, brood of vipers! How can you escape the condemnation of hell?" (Matthew 23:33)

Eternal damnation

Think about how easy it is to simply dismiss God and be tricked to follow Satan and this World's ways of doing things.

Hellfire

A place with nothing else but eternal torment. A place where there will be many who had believed in Jesus Christ but did not follow Him. Those who choose other religions and all the unbelievers will also be in this place.

All people have feelings.
Such as love, pleasure, happiness. They have joy, sorrow, ups, and downs. Most people live in their best state, in the lust of the flesh! All of these will be taken from them in the lake of fire.
-There is nothing else than eternal torment in that place. Forever.

No warning is too strong

To fall in the hands of the living God is something that at all costs must be avoided.

"And do not fear those who kill the body but cannot kill the soul. But rather fear Him who is able to destroy both soul and body in hell." (Matthew 10:28)

Steal - kill and destroy

Satan is here only to steal, to kill, and to destroy. When you read this scripture, it is easy to think that you shall lose everything, and everything you do shall be destroyed. And that is Satan's plan for you.

But think about all those around you that are wealthy. Do you ever think that Satan has the same plan for them? Yes, he does, but he uses a different strategy against these than you. (John 10:10)

Maybe your finances are low. Maybe many things are a struggle in your life. But you must hold on to the Lord and His promises. Perhaps it is difficult when you see the neighbors' big Mercedes and his wife that could be on any front cover. Maybe you'd think: he is not even saved, but he has all of these. What about me?

Satan has nothing against those people who are rich and are swimming in luxury. But what happens to these people after their life ends? Most of them will not enter the kingdom of God.

"Assuredly, I say to you that it is hard for a rich man to enter the kingdom of heaven." (Matthew 19:23)

Look at yourself, no one else
Give thanks to the Lord for what you already have. If you are standing in faith for a new house or car? Be blessed in Jesus' name.

"Giving thanks always for all things to God the Father in the name of our Lord Jesus Christ." (Ephesians 5:20)

Until now they have lost
We live in a constant battle, as the Bible says. Have all Christians understood this battle?
What about those who believe in God but are not born again? They live a peaceful life, but the truth is that they live in a constant defeat. A defeat that Satan controls through their feelings.

Jesus wants all of us to live our lives in victory. But the truth is that most of us are losers. Not losers like this world look at it, but someone who loses every day when Satan attacks us. He attacks us in ways that we do not understand, that's why we become losers.

Why are you running after your thoughts?
A thought comes to us, and we run after it. Maybe you are driving your car, and while you are driving, you are talking to the Lord, or perhaps you are just enjoying the lovely view.
Then it comes; you must check your load on your cell phone.

How do we respond to this kind of thought most of the time? We grab our cell phone to check how much load that is left. We leave the time we had with the Lord (or the nice view), we leave everything just to check our load. And when we do this, a feeling of satisfaction comes to us.

When you start to understand where these thoughts are coming from, it is now that you begin to reveal Satan and his strategies. We appeal too much to our emotions. That is why the Bible says that we shall not trust our feelings.
If you discern between the spirits, you reveal them. If you do not discern, you act on what comes to your mind.

"But I fear, lest somehow, as the serpent deceived Eve by his craftiness, so your minds may be corrupted from the simplicity that is in Christ." (2 Corinthians 11:3)

Seductions
We hear about it all the time. Churches - Congregations that have been seduced. False teaching, or perhaps the whole leadership, is false. It is very easy to accuse these churches, but maybe we shall start by looking on at ourselves in the mirror?
We are all personally responsible for knowing and obeying the written word of Almighty God.

If Jesus is your Lord, you will hear His voice
"My sheep hear My voice, and I know them, and they follow Me." (John 10:27)

Jesus speaks through His written word

You follow His written Word, not your feelings, experiences, and any of other people's perceptions and opinions.

No sin will enter heaven

Today, thousands of congregations are preaching the following; from the day you repented all of your sins, whatever you do after this is no longer a sin.

If you should lie or steal, or look at other with lust after you repent, it is only a human error because we are not perfect.

-This doctrine is 100% untrue and false.

Look what the Bible says about those who lie. What liars? All liars.

"But the cowardly, unbelieving, abominable, murderers, sexually immoral, sorcerers, idolaters, and all liars shall have their part in the lake which burns with fire and brimstone, which is the second death." (Revelation 21:8)

If you lie, you are a sinner in the Lord's eyes. Repentance from lying is what you need to do.

Renewed by the Holy Spirit

"But you have not so learned Christ, if indeed you have heard Him and have been taught by Him, as the truth is in Jesus; that you put off, concerning your former conduct, the old man which grows corrupt according to the deceitful lusts, and be renewed in your spirit of your mind." (Ephesians 4:20-23)

Take the Lord's word seriously. Be a winner over Satan and the demons.

Grab the victory and triumph in Jesus' name.

Notes;

_____

_____

_____

_____

_____

_____

_____

_____

_____

_____

164

Notes;

_____

_____

_____

_____

_____

_____

_____

_____

_____

_____

_____

CHAPTER 15

Holiness

Repent

What do you do most of your daily?

Is it your kingdom who is the Number one? Or is it God's king-dom that is Number one - in everything you are doing?

Be Holy in all manner of conversation

"Therefore gird up the loins of your mind, be sober, and rest your hope fully upon the grace that is to be brought to you at the revelation of Jesus Christ; as obedient children, not conforming yourselves to the former lusts, as in your ignorance; but as He who called you is holy, you also be holy in all your conduct, be-cause it is written, be holy for I am holy." (1 Peter 1:13-16)

The key is obedience

"As obedient children, not conforming yourselves to the former lusts, as in your ignorance." (1 Peter 1:14)

You shall be holy, for I am Holy. It is written.

"Pursue peace with all people, and holiness, without which no one will see the Lord." (Hebrews 12:14)

God called us not unto uncleanness, but unto sanctification.

"Therefore if anyone cleanses himself from the latter, he will be a vessel for honor, sanctified and useful for the Master, prepared for every good work." (2 Timothy 2:21)

Cleanse yourself from all filthiness of the flesh and spirit.

"For whatever is born of God overcomes the world. And this is the victory that has overcome the world - our faith." (1 John 5:4)

Die to sins and live for righteousness
"Or do you not know that your body is the temple of the Holy Spirit who is in you, whom you have from God, and you are not your own?" (1 Corinthians 6:19)

Your spiritual Liturgy
Prepare your bodies as a living and holy sacrifice, which is pleasing to God.

Be a doer of the word, and not hearers only
"Therefore lay aside all filthiness and overflow of wickedness, and receive with meekness the implanted word, which is able to save your souls." (James 1:21)

Whoever sticks to the Lord is one spirit with Him
"But shun profane and idle babblings, for they will increase to more ungodliness." (2 Timothy 2:16)

"For you were bought at a price; therefore, glorify God in your body and in your spirit, which are God's." (1 Corinthians 6:20)

We are a chosen one. A Royal Priesthood
"But you are a chosen generation, a royal priesthood, a holy nation, His own special people, that you may proclaim the praises of Him who called you out of darkness into His marvelous light; who once were not a people but are now the people of God, who had not obtained mercy but now have obtained mercy."
(1 Peter 2:9-10)

Sanctification
"Pursue peace with all people, and holiness, without which no one will see the Lord." (Hebrews 12:14)

"Therefore, laying aside all malice, all deceit, hypocrisy, envy, and all evil speaking." (1 Peter 2:1)

We must put down old corrupt and be renewed in mind and spirit
"Therefore, putting away lying, let each one of you speak the truth with his neighbor." (Ephesians 4:25)

The death sentence
You can not belong to Christ unless you crucify all self - indulgent passions and desires.

"And those who are Christ's have crucified the flesh with its passions and desires." (Galatians 5:24)

168

"Who Himself bore our sins in His own body on the tree, that we, having died to sins, might live for righteousness - by whose stripes you were healed." (1 Peter 2:24)

How does it look inside?
"When the Pharisee saw it, he marveled that He had not first washed before dinner. Then the Lord said to him, "Now you Pharisees make the outside of the cup and dish clean, but your inward part is full of greed and wickedness. Foolish ones! Did not He who made the outside make the inside also?" (Luke 11:38-40)

Unfortunately, many Christians work to wash, externally, to look good in the eyes of others.
-But within a dark carpet covers most of the light.

Quiet time
What is a quiet time in your room?

"But you, when you pray, go into your room, and when you have shut your door, pray to your Father who is in the secret place; and your Father who sees in secret will reward you openly." (Matthew 6:6)

Salary Chamber prayer means
Tranquility in the small room in the interior of man. It is easier to make this happen when it is quiet around you. As you practice, it will be easier and easier to find tranquility.
-This is not soaking or meditation.

Here we shall enter the Lord's presence, and in the sharpened state. Feel free to use earplugs and close your eyes. Now you are in a training camp with the Lord, and Satan hates you come through on this field. As described above, is this prayer tranquility in the interior. Then it's not a lot of prayers that shall come out of you but listen in silence as applicable.

While listening, it will come sneaking a lot of thoughts. All these we need to train to take captive to the obedience of Christ. (2 Corinthians 10:5)

Not a single thought you shall 'just' accept.

There in silence, that's where you will become more and more sensitive to hear the voice of God. This is where the Lord will train you in how to distinguish between the voices in your mind. It may take time to come through here, but never give up.

-Take up your daily cross and follow Jesus. (Matthew 16:24)

"Draw near to God, and he will draw near to you." (James 4:8)

Behind the curtain, that's where it happens

One day I preached in a church in the Philippines. There were several that asked me before the meeting how I had prepared myself for this day.

The truth was that I had prepared myself 'behind' the curtain in the Lord's presence.

I had prayed to the Lord for His presence and nothing else.

-Prayed for the Holy Spirit to move on the people who had come that day.

The meeting starts;

I began to give thanks to the Holy Ghost for His presence.

Then I started very low to sing Our Father, who art in heaven. I did not progress to the second verse, cause the Lord decided to show up.

Suddenly the whole church burst into tears.

I descended from the pulpit and stood on the side of the room and let God be God.

Most of the works behind the curtain are;

A daily surrender and decomposition of the flesh: A surrendered life to the Lord: an everyday life with quiet time with Him.

-Your surrendered life with the Lord brings victory.

"For the kingdom of God is not in word, but in power."
(1 Corinthians 4:20)

"He must increase, but I must decrease." (John 3:30)

The daily breakdown, live in it

Every day every week, 365 days a year, you must live in constant repentance. You did repent when you accepted Jesus, but repentance also means; think differently. Now your responsibility is to live - stay in the repentance.

This is what's going to be a challenge. Anywhere you go in this world: temptations will try to pull you in all directions. Therefore, it is essential and diligently to live in repentance.

-Think, do what God's Word says, not what this world means.

Your work may be in a place where most people are unsaved. The language and attitude of this world are just some of what you have listened to every single day.

If God is for us, who can be against us? (Romans 8:31)

-Resist the works of the flesh! (Galatians 5:19-21) And live in sanctification. (Ephesians 6:1-9)

Begin walking in the spiritual fruits. (Galatians 5:22-26)

"Because it is written, be holy, for I am holy." (1 Peter 1:16)

Humble yourself daily before the Lord.

For it is written;
"God resists the proud, but gives grace to the humble."
(James 4:6)

"Therefore submit to God. Resist the devil and he will flee from you." (James 4:7)

Do not be ignorant
"My people are destroyed for lack of knowledge." (Hosea 4:6)

In Greek, the word **ignorant: agneo** - it means; Ignore - not knowing because of lack of information or not understanding - not be aware.

Angry like a pitbull

Many times, in your life, you've probably been angry. Have you noticed that when you start to get angry, you get quick 'very' angry?

-This World says this; It is good to blow out some 'steam' now and then.

-The Bible has a different opinion on this.

Turn your minds on things above

"But now you yourselves are to put off all these; anger, wrath, malice, blasphemy, filthy language out of your mouth." (Colossians 3:8)

"Do not lie to one another, since you have put off the old man with his deeds, and have put on the new man who is renewed in knowledge according to the image of Him who created him." (Colossians 3:9-10)

Humbleness

"So then, my beloved brethren, let every man be swift to hear, slow to speak, slow to wrath; for the wrath of man does not produce the righteousness of God. Therefore, lay aside all filthiness and overflow of wickedness, and receive with meekness the implanted word, which is able to save your souls." (James 1:19-20)

"As new-born babes, desire the pure milk of the word, that you may grow thereby if indeed you have tasted that the Lord is gracious." (1 Peter 2:2-3)

"Therefore, whoever humbles himself as this little child is the greatest in the kingdom of heaven." (Matthew 18:4)

"Therefore, humble yourselves under the mighty hand of God, that He may exalt you in due time, casting all your care upon Him, for He cares for you." (1 Peter 5:6-7)

"Be diligent to present yourself approved to God, a worker who does not need to be ashamed, rightly dividing the word of truth." (2 Timothy 2:15)

"And Jesus said to them, I am the bread of life. He who comes to Me shall never hunger, and he who believes in Me shall never thirst." (John 6:35)

God's Word, believe it, take it, dare to act on it.

Notes:

_____

_____

_____

_____

_____

_____

174

Notes;

CHAPTER 16

God's promises

Rescue mission

Are you one who has been born again and baptized in the Holy Spirit?

-Then I have these following encouragements for you.

People are looking for solutions to everything at all levels. They are searching in their haystack and in other's haystacks for whatever reasons they are having.

But consider the following; You are one who has been given the power who said, **Let there be light, and there was light.**
This power lives inside of you. It is the same power that raised Jesus from the dead. It has taken residence in <u>you</u>.

Do we have anything to fear when the Lord says

Go into all the world and preach the gospel to every creature?
Go and heal the sick and set the oppressed free?

There is nothing impossible for the Holy Spirit to perform.

But are we living a surrendered life to the Lord for Him to use us?

Are we living a life that indicates that we are truly born again?
Do we take it seriously when the Lord told us to go?
Do we dare to travel independently to the other side of the
world, distributing food and preach the gospel to the poor?

Do we dare to believe when the Lord says: Go, I'm with you, I
will never leave you nor **forsake** you? (Hebrews 13:5)

We have read the word **forsake**. Forsake means from the Greek;
I will not leave you at any place.

Here the Lord points out the following; If you go into all the
world (Mark 16:15), He will be with you, and under no circumstances will he let go of you - leave you in any way.

This is a great challenge for you who read this
Yes, I choose to call it good, for it is my testimony in my Christian life.

Every time I have walked on water, the Lord has been with me.
I'll never forget the time I had a prayer line inside a Catholic
church just before they should have a mass, and everyone got
what they were offered. Healing.

Taking the plunge into the uncomfortable, you will get to know
the Lord.
-This is precisely where He wants you to be.

Look at Peter when he stood inside his safe boat, and Jesus came
walking on water. What a surprise and amazement it must have

been for those who were in the boat when they saw a man walking on the water in which they can't walk on.

I think all of us will be in the same state and said, Lord, is it you?
To top of it all, Jesus said, come.

It was not consistent in the water that made it possible for Peter to walk on water. It was solely God's promise that made it possible. The promise was then activated when Peter chose to believe and act on what Jesus has said, and not on his own opinions about water consistency.

This miracle is still talked about 2,000 years later. Jesus Christ has the same plan for you. Maybe you are not going to walk physically on the water, but this is a picture of the Lord unto you with a promise that signs and wonders will follow those who believe. If you go out in the uncomfortable unknowns; If you dare to use the courage that you have, then God Yahweh, the Creator of all things, will be with you as you walk on your journey.

God's promises
There is no greater promise in the whole universe than God's promises to humanity.
God's wonderful promises to you.
He wants an entirely personal and loving relationship with you more than what you can ever imagine.

God Yahweh gave His only begotten Son on the cross, so you and I would get the chance to be reconciled with God.

"He who forgives all your iniquities, who heals all your diseases." (Psalm 103:3)

"Delight yourself also in the Lord, and He shall give you the desires of your heart." (Psalm 37:4)

"If you abide in Me, and My words abide in you, you will ask what you desire, and it shall be done for you." (John 15:7)

"Therefore I say to you, whatever things you ask when you pray, believe that you receive them, and you will have them." (Mark 11:24)

"Now faith is the substance of things hoped for, the evidence of things not seen." (Hebrews 11:1)

"But when the kindness and the love of God our Savior toward man appeared, not by works of righteousness which we have done, but according to His mercy He saved us, through the washing of regeneration and renewing of the Holy Spirit, whom He poured out on us abundantly through Jesus Christ our Savior." (Titus 3:4-6)

"For where two or three are gathered together in My name, I am there in the midst of them." (Matthew 18:20)

Know the integrity of God's Word and act upon it.

2

-It will not fail you because God will never forsake you.

"The entrance of Your words gives light. It gives understanding to the simple." (Psalm 119:130)

"Casting all your care upon Him, for He cares for you."
(1 Peter 5:7)

"But without faith, it is impossible to please Him, for he who comes to God must believe that He is, and that He is a rewarder of those who diligently seek Him." (Hebrews 11:6)

Be a valiant believer
Do not let yourself be ruled by 'cannot' feelings and other infidel believers.
Let the Scripture tells you what to do, what to believe, and how to handle your faith.

The Lord has promised that He will never leave nor forsake you. (Hebrews 13:5)

Believe it, and dare to act on it.

If God has said it, then it will happen.
-God can not lie! (Titus 1:2)

All its 66 books are true. It is written.

"All Scripture is given by inspiration of God, and is profitable for doctrine, for reproof, for correction, for instruction in righteousness, that the man of God may be complete, thoroughly equipped for every good work." (2 Timothy 3:16-17)

When God speaks, it is the truth itself that speaks. What He says will happen by all means.

Noah built an arc - God flooded. (Genesis 6:14, 7:17-21)
Moses obeyed - God divided the waters. (Exodus 14:21)
Joshua marched - God tore down the wall. (Joshua 6:20)
Elijah struck the water - God divided the waters. (2 Kings 2:8)
Naaman dipped seven times in the Jordan River - God healed leprosy. (2 Kings 5:14)
Jesus said that the believer who lay his hands on the sick - God will heal. (Mark 16:18)

God can not lie
Obey what God tells you to do, expect God to do what He says He will do. That is faith.

Accept that God's word is true and begin to act on it, just as what the early Christians did.
The disciples laid their hands on the sick, and the Lord healed the sick.
-We shall do the same.

Do not trust your feelings. God's words are better than your feelings.
Believe that His words will win all the time.

The universe's biggest promise

"For God so loved the world that he gave his only begotten Son, that whoever believes in Him should not perish, but have everlasting life." (John 3:16)

Notes;

_____

_____

_____

_____

_____

_____

_____

_____

_____

182

Notes;

_____

_____

_____

_____

_____

_____

_____

_____

_____

_____

_____

CHAPTER 17

Give, and it shall be given to you

If you must be a giver, then your wallet must be opened, not just be ajar. The one, who is a giver, is someone who has God's passionate cause burning in their lives. Many are givers, but do we give where we shall give?

Many are giving to the one who shouts loudest, and others give to the ones with the 'biggest' ministries with private jets. There is one thing that I have mentioned many times in this book, and that is the Lord's Gospel to a lost world. But sad to say, not many Christians believe they shall be a doer of the word when it becomes to this matter.

Those who do not 'believe,' have an excellent opportunity to be a faithful supporters of those who are willing to go into the world with the Gospel of Jesus Christ.
The Lord wants everybody to come to the knowledge of truth and be saved. Therefore, those who are willing to go into the world must get much more attention than what they do today.

Move into a position with your life where you become a person who is acting on what is written in Romans 10:13-15.

"For whoever calls on the name of the Lord shall be saved. How then shall they call on Him in whom they have not believed? And how shall they believe in Him of whom they have not heard? And how shall they hear without a preacher? And how shall they preach unless they are **sent**? As it is written, How beautiful are the feet of those who preach the Gospel of peace, who bring glad tidings of good things!"

The word **sent** means from the Greek; Sent out on a mission.

You can be with those and give help to those when it comes to larger or smaller projects.
There is nothing greater than feet that bring the Lord's Gospel to the lost.

"So let each one give as he **purposes** in his heart, not grudgingly or of necessity; for God loves a cheerful (willing) giver."
(2 Corinthians 9:7)

We read the word **purposes**. It is from the Greek word **proaire-omai**, it means; To choose for oneself before another thing.

Here, you need to make a choice. Are you going to equip those who are willing to go into the world, or are your wishes and desires more important?

The Gospel to a lost world.
To those who lay down their lives, those who stand daily in the spiritual battle for the unsaved, the poor, the defeated shall be

reached with the Gospel. Yes, they need the support of those who are 'at home.'

"But do not forget to do good and to **share**, for, with such sacrifices, God is well pleased." (Hebrews 13:16)

The word **share** is from the Greek language; Partnership, fellowship.

"Give, and it will be given to you: good measure, pressed down, shaken together, and running over will be put into your bosom. For with the same measure that you use, it will be measured back to you." (Luke 6:38)

We must take care of the weak
We give because it is more blessed than to receive. (Acts 20:35) The world today is the total OPPOSITE of what is written in Acts 20:35.

Take a look at what the Bible says in the book of James
"If a brother or sister is naked and destitute of daily food, and one of you says to them, Depart in peace, be warmed and filled, but you do not give them the things which are needed for the body, what does it profit?" (James 2:15-16)

Your jacket
Imagine a leather jacket having the most excellent quality. By plainly looking at it, you can imagine how good and the representative you would be wearing it. You like the color, the details,

and the smell. There is absolutely nothing with it that you do not like.

Imagine the following
When Jesus Christ says: "Go" then you have to go. When Jesus says, "Give," then you have to give.
Think of all those who are struggling that will get.

This is how the Lord is trying to tell us how our minds must be set towards others.
-Not a second-class help, but a first-class help.
-Not bad rice to the hungry, but quality rice to such.
-Not cheap meat, but good meat.
-Not a diluted Gospel, but a mighty Gospel.

The jacket was very stylish to look at. It represents something.
-You, as a representative of the Lord among the lost, should be the one that comes with something.

When we believe and act on it.
Give to others what you want. Maybe you and your family at Christmas have turkey or something else. For many people, this time of the year is a time where we come together.
Next time, try to go out to the poor and give them what you want for Christmas.
-Go to those who do not have much.
Give to others what you want yourself.

We are all called by the Lord to be givers. Givers to those who are in need. Give so that you can feel it, not just a little bit.

It is not only money that we shall give; give of what you have, your wardrobe, your fridge, and so on.
If we have two jackets, we shall give the one to someone who needs it.

Humanitarian work

Give woolen blankets to those who freeze at night. To those who sleep on a bench, to those who have nothing in their lives.
Those who are empty, for everything.
-They need a helping hand; A hand that stretches out full of love.

The Gospel of Jesus Christ shall be given to those who lie there empty.

What Jesus did on Calvary was a giant rescue operation. If the Lord set the standard for a rescue mission, then why are Christians not attending the rescue work?

Jesus gave everything that man could be reconciled with God.
We give so that our bank account shall be bigger. Why?
-Selfishness, arrogance, and so on.

People die every day from starvation, from hunger, from violence and from cold. Most of them are not saved either.
Today's worldview is very serious. That makes it all more serious about being a Christian.

What does humanitarian means?

Good - Benevolent - Human - Human loving - Human-friendly - Mild - Beneficent - Charitable.

This is for all that are born again.

All of us must be humanitarian. All the words above you will find in the Bible.

Human Loving

You who is full of the Holy Ghost.

You. Who is loving the Lord with all your heart, all your mind, and soul.

You have to travel where the needs are significant, reaching out your hands and demonstrate God's kingdom.

Teaching about the sins of this world, repentance from it, and God's love through Jesus Christ.

-Give food to the hungry; Heal the sick, and set the oppressed free.

Donate happily to someone who does excellent work, but do not forget yourself in the great work.

Giving to the poor

The Bible talks a lot about giving to the poor. If you misinterpret these scriptures, it leads quickly to a condemnation of the poor.

Standard comments

If you only give to 'those,' they are just even lazier, and they will not work at all.

This must surely be a stunning example of how to judge others. Through this kind of statements, they try to justify themselves, so they do not need to do anything. Christians have and will always have an opinion about things.

This is to most of the time, to exalt their work, whatever it is.

When it comes to giving to the poor, Christians need to open their eyes.

The Lord says to all that are born again; Go out and make disciples of them.
Most of the time, we say, uh, the church has a course in discipleship.

The Lord says; Take care to those who are weak in faith.
We say, uh, how come?

The Lord says; Give them food.
We say; If we give them food, they become lazy and will not work. What they need is a fishnet so they can learn to get their food.
This is great and wonderful words that do not belong anywhere else in disobedience and laziness camp.
Those who come with these statements do not know the God of the Bible at all!

They confess but denies
"They profess to know God, but in works they deny Him, being abominable, disobedient, and disqualified for every good work." (Titus 1:16)

We prioritize and are always looking for alternatives. The only option is the Lord's commandments.
It is all right in front of us.

It is written

There is only one way to eternity in heaven.

"Jesus said to him, I am the way, the truth, and the life. No one comes to the Father except through Me." (John 14:6)

Self-centered egoists and better knowers have no place in God's kingdom.
-But God gives grace to the humble. (James 4:6)

Space

NASA uses billions of dollars every year for their space programs. But in the nearby cities and towns, there are thousands of homeless.
How can we defend this before God Almighty?

The Lord says; Give to the poor

We say; It's a separate budget. We need to go to Mars.

A world without Jesus Christ is a lost world.

He gave, and He was given

One time I saw a TV program about a man who gave sandwiches, clothes, and blankets to those who lived in the streets in a city in the U.S.A.
This man lived in a simple apartment in the same city, and every night around 9 pm, he filled his minivan and headed for the streets. He drove the same route every night after he had filled his van with sandwiches, woolen blankets, and other items that we take for granted.

But when you looked around inside his home, it was different.
People have big sofas and an enormous flat-screen on the wall.

All of this was substituted with 5-6 large freezers. Freezers that was filled with food to give to others.

He was a retired man, and he used all of his time and money to give to those who have not.
And what does he give? He gave his time, he gave his heart, his money, and every night he traveled to 70 different places in that city.
He kept it going until 9 am the next morning. Also, he struggled with various diseases.

The reporter who interviewed him, who was also with him the whole night, asked him a fascinating question. Why do you do all of this stuff?
-The man answered; God says in the Bible to help those who have nothing, **and I have something to give**.

When you begin to act on what the scripture says, the Holy Ghost can start His training of you. (John 14:26)
-His entire car was filled with something to give.

The Bible says, give, and it shall be given unto you
I would tell, we think primarily of money in this context. And yes, you need money, but does it starts with money?
Does it start that one sits in front of the Lord and begs for some Dollars so you can be a giver?
No, this is not how it starts.

Give, and it will be given unto you.
Is it money first? Think now before you answer.

Or do you need to be trained in how to do this? I am sure the Lord waits for you to start walking so He can begin His training of you.

So many times we give, just to get, without involving us.

Let us take a look at one word in Luke 6:38.
The word give. This word means; To minister, tell, allocate, give, show.

This is a simple picture of a giver. As you see, it is not only about money.
-But your surrendered life, your daily sanctification, your obedience to the Lord's commandments, will raise others to victory in Jesus Christ.

Let us read the whole of Luke 6:38 one more time. And this time, with eyes that know it has something to give, no matter what size of your wallet.

"Give, and it will be given to you: a good measure, pressed down, shaken together, and running over will be put into your bosom. For with the same measure that you use, it will be measured back to you."

The helping ministry is a test of authenticity.
(2 Corinthians 9:6-15)

The Lord says that we will have an abundance for every good work.

Do not think about all that you need. Start walking - that is the key.

Maybe you do not have faith in a vast ministry, with hundreds of people that need help every day.
But look at what is written in Mark 16:17: signs will follow those who believe.

"He who has two tunics, let him give to him who has none; and he who has food, let him do likewise." (Luke 3:11)

We just...need
We must reach what is on our daily agenda. We need that sofa, that iPhone, that flat-screen TV. Yes, we need the whole mail order catalog.

We always strive for more, while those who do not have food to give to their little ones who sit around the table, each with their blue and pink food bowl. Just let them sit there...with empty stomachs.

We close our eyes to the third world. Or shall we call it the **needy world?**
Or have we misunderstood something here? If you have a roof over your head and food every day, you have what you need. Do you see it?

The party is soon over
Parts of the world gorge themselves on food.
-More than 20 000 children die from poverty every single day.
This happens, and we accept it.

If you know the truth, but will not go - live - work in it, you sin.

"Therefore, to him who knows to do good and does not do it, to him it is a sin!" (James 4:17)

Notes;

_____

_____

_____

_____

_____

_____

_____

CHAPTER 18

God's patience is not eternal
Part 1

You may have someone in your family or from your circle of friends that is not saved. Perhaps the retirement is right around the corner, and the Lord they have their own opinions about. Or perhaps, it is you who are reading this now it concerns?

The Bible says that no man knows when they will leave this planet. Therefore, it is important to begin taking the Lord and His written Word seriously now.

Take it very seriously what the scripture says about the Lord
"And do not fear those who kill the body but cannot kill the soul. But rather fear Him who is able to destroy both soul and body in hell." (Matthew 10:28)

Your decision - Your repentance - The Lord is waiting.

Not now, later I will reconcile with God
You're maybe one who had a long life here on earth. Life in which you have been living <u>without</u> God.
You may think that there is a God. Maybe, you have prayed to a 'god.'

Perhaps you have lied, stolen something, committed adultery, etc. The list is maybe long.

A sinful life is what you have lived here on earth.

-In Gods' eyes, you are guilty of sin and will be judged accordingly.

The Bible says; There is not one just

"For there is not a just man on earth who does good and does not sin." (Ecclesiastes 7:20)

The Lord is very clear in His statement when It comes to human sins;

"For the wages of sin is death, but the gift of God is eternal life in Christ Jesus our Lord." (Romans 6:23)

Away from sin

For you to come into a relationship with the Lord and gain entry into the Kingdom of heaven, only God's Holy Bible shows the way to Him.

God has been put in a cubicle

A cubicle that you have built and put God in it. Man has made religion the moment he creates a god to meet his own needs and opinions. That God does, unfortunately, does not exists, only inside your head.

It is Almighty God who created all things

All the planets and entire cosmos included you. The Lord has been so personal with His creation, that the whole thing is simply unique. The animal and the plant life in which no scientist can explain anything of how it is created.

People do not believe, cause they do not see
Man does not believe if they cannot see it. They do not believe in God because they cannot see him. They think they are intelligent just because they can easy resonate simply and say; God does not exist; I cannot see him.

The Bible says that God is a spirit. Can we see a spirit? No, but that's because the Bible says that we cannot see God.

Then I have a question for you
Have you ever seen the wind?
-The wind is also invisible and just as real as Almighty God.

Humanity does all sorts of things, apart from having a living relationship with God
-They do not believe in God.
But if there was no God, it had not been necessary to pronounce: There is no God.

All people have eternity inside themselves
God has done something unique. He has imposed in their hearts enough truth to come to faith in Him.

We read in the Bible
"He has made everything beautiful in its time. Also, He has put eternity in their hearts, except that no one can find out the work that God does from beginning to end." (Ecclesiastes 3:11)

Here we see that you have enough of eternity inside you to take it.

-Lay down all your pride now.

Scripture says that we cannot add as much as an inch of our lives

That means; You never know when you're going to die.

The Bible says, "And which of you by worrying can add one cubit to his stature?" (Luke 12:25)

A cubit is an ancient unit of measurement, and it is a picture of time. Not a single second, we can add or subtract to our lives.

The Bible says

"Your eyes saw my substance, being yet unformed. And in Your book they all were written, the days fashioned for me. When as yet there were none of them." (Psalm 139:16)

God has complete control. He has determined all your days

When you leave this world, the Bible says in Hebrew 9:27; And it is appointed for men to die once, but after this the judgment.

Judgment day that you will never escape

The Lord has appointed it, and no sinner will never enter the Kingdom of God.

Judgment day is God's judgment over sin

"For the wages of sin is death, but the gift of God is eternal life in Christ Jesus our Lord." (Romans 6:23)

He who denies God is a fool
"The fool has said in his heart, there is no God!" (Psalm 14:1)

God can in a simple way lose patient with you and end your life
-Maybe you don't believe He would do such a thing?

Let us read Genesis 38:7 to see how God killed an evil man.

"But Er, Judah's firstborn, was wicked in the sight of the Lord, and the Lord killed him." (Genesis 38:7)

Jesus told about a man who boasted that he had so many goods that he would build bigger barns
Just as humans today. Builds and tear down, build some more, accumulating more. I need a new car and some more new things.

Do not try to think now
But I need the....!
Yes, God knows you need various things to survive. But it's most of the goods that have become your God.
That's what you are thinking, collecting, working for all the time.

It is severe what the Bible says here
"Then He spoke a parable to them, saying: The ground of a certain rich man yielded plentifully. And he thought within himself, saying, what shall I do since I have no room to store my crops? So he said, I will do this: I will pull down my barns and build greater, and there I will store all my crops and my goods.

And I will say to my soul, soul you have many goods laid up for many years; take your ease: eat, drink, and be merry. But God said to him, fool! This night your soul will be required of you; then whose will those things be which you have provided? **So is he who lays up treasure for himself, and is not rich toward God.**" (Luke 12:16-21)

-God called the man a fool and took his life that night.

We have replaced a relationship with God with material things.
The whole thing has become an idol.
Those who said that they should repent in their own time, **lacking the fear of the Lord.**

Their understanding of His nature is incorrect.
If they got a glimpse of His Holiness and His justice, then they would not take lightly on His grace.

The Lord will confront such arrogance.

He is not wise if he thinks that he can outwit his Creator, enjoying life in sin and repent at the last minute.

Notes;

_____

_____

_____

CHAPTER 19

God's patience is not eternal
Part 2

Deathbed repentance is rare

Many believe that it is easy to be saved within the eleventh hour.
That means to receive salvation just before you die.
However, this is a very selfish way of thinking when the Lord
looks at our hearts and not at the last minute's statements.

"For the time has come for judgment to begin at the house of
God; and if it begins with us first, what will be the end of those
who do not obey the gospel of God? Now if the righteous one is
scarcely saved, where will the ungodly and the sinner appear?"
(1 Peter 4:17-18)

Here, we can see that speculating to be saved in the 'eleventh'
hour, is not recommended.

Man

A Man lies. A man steals. A man makes their rules about God. A
man has lots of opinions about God, but do not know Him.
If you do not know God, then how dare people have an opinion
on how He acts?

Most people think that they will escape the judgment day.
-They won't! According to the scripture.

Let's take an example
You tried to steal a car, and you were caught in the act.
The police bring you to jail where you stay for a short time. Later, you have to appear in court. The day comes, and you will stand in front of a judge. This judge is a just judge, and he must judge according to the laws in the country you are.

For example - in the country of Norway, to steal cars is not allowed. So what will the judge do?
The police caught you in the act trying to steal a car, so the evidence is valid. The judge will judge you guilty, and you will have a penalty.
Maybe you have all kinds of excuses under your sleeves during the trial, but the evidence is clear, and the judge is a just judge.
-You are guilty.

The exact scenario will happen to you on judgment day
God is a just God. He cannot lie or be dishonest. You will be judged guilty if you have sins in your life, which remained unrepented.

God knows everything at all times
The Bible says that the Lord knows even the number of your hair in your head. (Matthew 10:30)

God has total control
It is only you who does not believe in it.

People are good at lying

Lying is something which people are very good at. Even a color map has been created over the years.

These are white lies, gray lies, rescue lie, so forth and so on.

Satan fills our heads with everything that goes against the word of God. If the Bible says that you shall not lie, then there is no reason to lie at all.

-The Lord says no, but people love to listen to Satan. They lie so much that they believe it themselves.

Satan does this solely because he knows that no liar will enter the kingdom of heaven.

You believe the thought that says, white lies are ok.

-Satan laughs; You die as we all shall one day, but you do not enter heaven.

This is what the Bible says about liars

"But the cowardly, unbelieving, abominable, murderers, sexually immoral, sorcerers, idolaters, and **all liars** shall have their part in the lake which burns with fire and brimstone, which is the second death." (Revelation 21:8)

God could not be clearer on this issue

All the liars will be judged according to God's standard. Just as how a car thief is being convicted before a just judge.

God is not different today than several thousand years ago. Nor in the future will He ever change His written Word.

-It is written;
"Jesus Christ is the same yesterday, today, and forever."
(Hebrews 13:8)

But God has created something stunning - and that is salvation.

Jesus Christ, man's only way to salvation
"Nor is there salvation in any other, for there is no other name under heaven given among men by which we must be saved." (Acts 4:12)

The Lord desires that all people turn away from sin and be saved.

Let us read 1 Timothy 2:3-4.
"God our Savior, who desires all men to be saved and to come to the knowledge of the truth."

God saw that humanity was sinful and made a rescue plan
This universe's biggest rescue mission was initiated 2000 years ago. It was Jesus Christ who bore all the sin to the cross and nailed it once and for all.

"Having wiped out the handwriting of requirements that was against us, which was contrary to us. And He has taken it out of the way, having nailed it to the cross. Having disarmed principalities and powers, He made a public spectacle of them, triumphing over them in it." (Colossians 2:14-15)

This made it possible for you and me, to come to God with our sin, repent of it, and trust Him for our salvation.

Lay down all your pride, repent from **all** sin in your life now, wait no longer.

There is only one way to heaven
"I am the way, the truth, and the life. No one comes to the Father except through Me." (John 14:6)

Repent means;
Stop doing, turn away from.

God, in His greatness, does not tolerate sin. But He loved humanity so much that He gave His only begotten Son on the cross so that you and I would have the opportunity to turn away from our sinful lives, and to Him. (John 3:16)

God has created you with a spirit and a soul. This cannot be destroyed, therefore forever in heaven, or eternal in hell.

It has, for years, been taught by priests and leaders around the world, about a place called purgatory.
-Let us take a look.

Purgatory
According to Catholic doctrine, (which publishes the catechism) is purgatory a caching state - place after physical death. Those who are destined for heaven, they undergo purification, to achieve holiness and enter the joy of heaven. Those who have

not achieved in life a sufficient level of sanctity can repent from this in purgatory.

-No one who comes to purgatory will ever come to hell.

The Bible says

"And as it is appointed for men to die once, but after this the judgment." (Hebrews 9:27)

Out of this scripture, we can see that purgatory does not exist.

-Think about it. Jesus died for all the sinners. And all the sinners must repent of all their sins to be saved, while they are still alive here on earth. If you die without repentance from what the Bible says is a sin, you will miss salvation.

The Lord says we for sure one time shall die, and then judgment will come after. The Bible does not say anything about a place after death that you can repent further in.

-The first thing that will happen after your death is judgment.

Do not wait any longer. Repent all your sins, and turn back to the Lord. You never know when you pull your last breath of air here on earth.

-The Lord is waiting.

"For the scripture says,
whoever believes in Him (Jesus) will not be put to shame." (Romans 10:11)

Confess all your sins to God
Trust Christ for your salvation, and you will pass from death to life.
-You have God's promise on it.

Call on Jesus Christ right now
He will hear you if you approach Him with a humble and sorrowful heart.

The Bible says there is joy in heaven when sinners repent. (Luke 15:7)

God gave everything so you and He would get a chance to be reunited
"For God so loved the world that He gave His only begotten Son, that whoever believes in Him should not perish but have everlasting life." (John 3:16)

True repentance is the only door opener to Jesus Christ.

Remember that God knows everything that you have said, what you have thought, and what you have done in your life.

Pray something like this;

Dear Jesus!
I thank you that you gave your life for me on the cross.
Jesus, I want now to become a child of God.
Forgive me for all the wrong I have done.

Forgive me that I have lied, committed adultery, stolen, and all the sinful acts that I've done.

Forgive me that I have not lived life together with you.

-Forgive me, Jesus, that I have sinned against you.

If you choose this, you go from death to life.

-I thank you, Jesus, that I am now forgiven for all the wrong and bad things that I have done in life.

-I thank you, Jesus, that I am now a child of God. In Jesus' Name, Amen.

It is now it all starts

It is from now you must build your relationship with God.

The Bible is God's written word and guidelines for you.

-Start to read it every day.

Every day, pray to Him. There are no fixed ways to pray to Him, but talk to Him and end it in Jesus' name.

Praying to God means to have a conversation with God. There is a time to talk and a time to listen.

"Now this is the confidence that we have in Him, that if we ask anything according to His will, He hears us. And if we know that He hears us, whatever we ask, we know that we have the petitions that we have asked of Him." (1 John 5:14-15)

Let God be God when you pray. Let Him train you up, be humble in front of Him.

Begin to witness to others what the Lord has done in your life. This is crucial for the Holy Ghost to be able to teach you all things. (John 14:26)

There is victory in Jesus' Name!

Notes;

_____

_____

_____

_____

_____

_____

_____

210

Notes;

_____

_____

_____

_____

_____

_____

_____

_____

_____

_____

_____

_____

CHAPTER 20

Thank you very much for reading this book

I hope it has been an inspiration to you, and that you will take the plunge into the power ministry our Lord and Savior Jesus Christ has for you. It is essential to get into a Biblical understanding of who our God is.

Lay down your life, surrender everything to the Lord our God. He said that signs and wonders will follow those who believe.

All the old, all of the carnal desires, everything that goes against the Lord's written Word, must be repented from in your life.

All knowledge that you need in your life must come from the Lord. He will give to all who are willing to lay down their lives in this world, and obey His commandments.

Take it, seek the Lord with all your heart, with all your strength, with all your mind.
Then you will have it.

Stay updated

There are new books on its way. Stay tuned to our website for new releases.

www.SecretRevelations.com

May the Lord bless you and yours abundantly.

Author - Rune Larsen

Pain or any sickness, be healed in Jesus name!

.

www.ingramcontent.com/pod-product-compliance
Lightning Source LLC
LaVergne TN
LVHW022322080426
835508LV00041B/1743